WE CAME BACK TO SAY

An Anthology of Memoir

Edited by
Theo Pauline Nestor

Permissions:

The essay "A Person of Color" by Sandy Barnes was originally published in a different form on Outwardlink.net in January, 2012.

Wendy Staley Colbert's "Bearing Max" was originally published on ParentMap.com.

We Came Back to Say © 2012 by Theo Pauline Nestor
The stories in the anthology are © 2012 of the respective authors.

All rights reserved.
Published in the United States by
Theo Pauline Nestor
No part of this book may be reproduced in any manner whatsoever without prior written permission of the individual authors, except in the case of brief quotations embodied in critical articles or reviews.

Cover illustration used with permission of the artist, Anthony Russo © 2012

Book and Cover design: Vladimir Verano, Third Place Press

ISBN: 978-1-60944-063-3

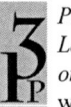
Printed and bound at Third Place Press,
Lake Forest Park, WA
on the Espresso Book Machine v.2.2.
www.thirdplacepress.com

TABLE OF CONTENTS

Introduction	Theo Pauline Nestor	1
How to Be Analog	by Natalie Singer	3
Pieces of Me	by Deli Moussavi-Bock	12
French Maids	by Paul Boardman	19
Chemistry	by Jeanne Verville	27
Bearing Max	by Wendy Staley Colbert	33
My Greek Father, a Bacon Cheeseburger Deluxe, and a Boy from Queens	by Elizabeth M. Economou	38
Finished	by Kellini Walter	43
Me, My Weight, and I	by Dana Montanari	50
Fishing in Death Valley	by Jennifer Crowder	58
Mama and Her Liquor License	by Eleanor Owen	66
Probabilities of Love and Cancer	by Christiane Banta	74
Lessons Still Learning: I Once Was Lost but Now I'm Found	by Peggy A. Nagae	82
Bodhisattva in Training	by Faren Bachelis	90
The Upside of Loss	by Star Roberts	97
A Person of Color	by Sandy Barnes	104

TABLE OF CONTENTS, *CONTINUED*

The Moth of Mirth	by Julie Parks	111
Eat Me	by John Mace	115
My Federal Trade Commission Testimony	by Johna Beall	122
Finding Don Cameron	by Sue Wiedenfeld	130
A Cosmic Shift in Utah	by Robyne L. Curry	138
The Cookie Scholarship	by Jean Engler	146
Dee's Loft	by Joyce Tomlinson	152
Something Clicks into Place	by Carmen D'Arcangelo	157
A Taste of Home	by Amber Wong	160
End of the Line	by Linda Zbigley	167
Contributors		175

Introduction

WHAT'S RISKIER THAN WRITING ABOUT YOUR OWN EXPERIENCES, thoughts, and feelings? Putting your story out there for the world to read with the "Memoir" stamp upon it that declares to the world "Yes, this happened to me and this is how I see it."

For the last six years that I've been teaching memoir writing for the University of Washington's Professional and Continuing Education Program I've had the opportunity to work closely with a new group of emerging memoir writers each year. Many of those students—including many of the writers here in *We Came Back to Say*—have continued to work with me individually after the nine-month course has ended. Watching these writers evolve and push themselves to take greater risks in their writing has been a tremendous joy for me as a teacher.

I'm thrilled now to be sharing new work from this group of emerging writers with you.

Enjoy!

Theo Pauline Nestor

HOW TO BE ANALOG

By Natalie Singer

First, your dad has to have a *really large* collection of records that he keeps perfectly preserved and always accessible, lined up tight, soft paper spines facing out on the bottom shelf of the wall unit in a row that seems to stretch forever.

When you drag your hand down this row it is neat and solid, like a wall. Wedge a tiny finger under one record case and gently lift it a bit from its place in the order: it feels pleasantly heavy, and it drops back down into the row with a satisfying "click" like when you snap your tongue on the roof of your mouth, which is a trick you just learned after practicing for-EVER.

The records belong to your father, but they are your mother's, too. They are all of yours, as a pet is or a baby.

When you are very small, and it is just the three of you, you will be sticky and uncomfortable from the Florida heat and shimmy out of bed and your father and mother will be lounging around the living room on the brown nubby couch in their terry cloth shorts drinking Coca Cola, maybe smoking some pot, with the windows wide open and they will place the giant black headphones comically over your frizzy hair and eager ears and hand you a microphone and you will belt out Beach Boys or Bee Gees and twirl in your Strawberry Shortcake nightgown while the skinny palms sweat the night away outside.

You will listen to whatever your father has in his collection, which includes: Stevie Wonder just calling to say he loves you, Bruce Springsteen calling everybody out for having a hungry heart, and The Eagles forecasting a heartache tonight.

· *We Came Back to Say* ·

The music sounds like summer nights, cotton candy, roller skates on blacktop; it reminds you of when The Tide is High and that We Are Family and it also makes you wonder what exactly *is* a Hot Child in the City? It is black afros and white afros and sunglasses and disco balls and chocolate milkshakes and drive-ins and your fifteen-year-old mother's dried school-dance corsage and rounded-block fonts and tight-ass Sassoons and your dad's baby blue wedding tuxedo and triangle bikinis and trips to your favorite place on Earth, Disney World, where at the family fun farm you pet a deer and in the sepia-toned picture that results the bright white of your jeans is mirrored in the white spots on the deer's tail.

Music sings through car speakers: your mom's long, low, wood-paneled station wagon as you cruise the Publix parking lot; your dad's door-less, bird-blue Jeep CJ, bumping your tiny butt to nursery school.

Saturday is American Bandstand, and you all gather around the TV with your orange juice, your father in his Jew 'fro and brown Top-Siders and pink Lacoste T-shirt and your mother in that long, mustard-colored jersey dress, skinny and sunburned. Dick Clark comes on in his own pink shirt and the dancers, young and cool like your parents, crowd the stage. They boogie on and on.

Later, much later and no matter where you are, when you close your eyes you will always be able to see the packed dance floor of American Bandstand. You will smell the ash of your parents' Marlboros tapped into tiger's eye ashtrays; the wet of a swamp monsoon; your mother's Chanel perfume and pink Bubbleicious chewing gum and lemony Mr. Clean.

Later you will see, too, the wooden wall unit set up in a new house thousands of miles from any palm trees; a baby brother, then another; the same long row of records plus some fresh ones loaded with songs about Billie Jean, uptown girls, material girls, and how everybody wants to rule the world.

One night you will see your father arrive home after work in his camelhair suit, your mother vexed because it is late and she has cranky kids and deep inside she is still one of those girls who just wanna have fun, but then the shiny new 45 finds its way out of his briefcase and onto the record player.

"Cyndi Lauper," your dad grins, his eyebrows lifting, and you all look at each other excitedly: *What* is this?

To be analog you will handle your father's records if you are very careful, even though you are only four and five, because for now your baby brothers don't exist and no one has taken it on the run, and it is just you and them and they are young and happy and just let her do it, she is *such* a good girl.

First, you check the cover. All the colors in the world are on a record cover. Record albums, they are properly called. That go on the *turntable*, your grandparents say. Often it's a picture of the group, in outrageous clothes, with many instruments and flowing hair, and you feel you could study the cover forever, maybe crawl inside.

You gently squeeze the cardboard envelope so that the slit in the middle bows a little. It has to make an arc that is the curve of a banana, maybe a smidge less, nothing more. Then a small shake, and the record slides out. Catch it with your small right hand. Hold it like a plate.

The vinyl, an LP, is not too heavy, not too light, an ebony disc encoded with hidden language. Precise, comforting, perfect every time. Its spiral groove makes a funny *zip* under your fingernail that tingles up your arm. Of course you don't scratch it.

If you are unsure how to adjust for a 33 or a 45, your dad will show you. They are all of your records, but really they are his. *He* is the curator, the collector, the connoisseur.

Put it on. Slowly, lower the center of the record's colored label onto the spindle. Watch the rounded silver nub push gently through the tiny hole. The record and the *turntable* coupling, but you don't know about all that yet.

Lift the arm, gently, lower the needle to the record's outer edge (maybe you have a button and all this happens automatically). There will be static crackle for a couple of seconds. Wait.

The music wafts. You and your mother dance, snapping your fingers, shaking your stuff, but your dad sits on the couch, ankles crossed, hands tucked quietly under his thighs, and rocks. The songs, often pop but also classic rock and the tail end of disco, put your father into a kind of appreciatory trance; they pass through him and leave the space around him altered. More than anything, he is perhaps a medium, not so different from his buddy Ruby who is into transcendental meditation and comes over to breathe and levitate alone in your cool, dark basement.

To be analog you need your father's records, but, of course, you also have your own.

Your first record player, before you can speak, is a Fisher Price toy with plastic, ice-cream-colored discs that play lullabies.

Your first *real* record player is built into a red-and-white, candy-striped box with a latching lid. You carefully select your record and lower it into the peppermint cavity. When you get bored, you switch out for another album. You dust and sort and store everything with care. You are three.

Your next record player is caramel brown, with a carrying handle. It lasts you a long time.

You have Raffi; Sharon, Lois & Bram; Sesame Street Disco Fever; The Wizard of Oz; Peter, Paul and Mommy; Cinderella; The Jackson 5; and of course your favorite: the special 45 your parents bought you in Disney, a commemorative picture disc of synthesizer-created parade music that you listen to for hours and hours.

You have forgotten none of it, not a single song, although it takes some work to remember.

How to Flex Your Musical Muscle Memory

Musical memories are stored in part of the brain known as the medial prefrontal cortex, which lives just behind the forehead. New scientific research has shown that the music and songs identified by study subjects as triggering the strongest memories from their lives are the same tunes that, when played, show up in brain scans as spikes of mental activity in the medial prefrontal cortex. Music-tracking activity in the brain is also stronger during more powerful autobiographical memories. Experts think the research explains why even Alzheimer's patients with increasing memory loss can still recall songs from their distant past.

You wonder if this might work one day on your mother, who is sick now, who cannot dance or even walk, whose memories, and thoughts, sometime slur.

To exercise the powers of your own musical muscle memory, you must be on at all times, open for reception, your musical ear like a kind of radar that might power down but never turns off.

You will be driving in the car and some old song comes on and suddenly it overtakes you, the realness of your memories, the feeling of *I am not here, I am* **there** *right now but how is that possible because* **there** *is long gone but I feel it, and it feels* **so real**. It is all you can do to keep your hands on the wheel and the tires on the road.

This happens every week or two or four.

To understand music, we must understand memory. Like:

When you are twelve you are supposed to go to a concert with your father. You two never go anywhere alone anymore, because you live with your mom and see him only on weekends with your brother. But because he loves music you are not too surprised when you ask him to take you to see George Michael and he agrees.

You try not to think of the tradeoff, the awkwardness that will surely come with standing next to your father and trying to pretend the words to your favorite song, "I Want Your Sex," are not embarrassing, that they are simply letters of the alphabet strung together which explain facts of life both you and your father can accept and understand.

The night before the concert, your dad calls.

"Hi honey, ready for George Michael?"

"Yeah, should be good," you murmur, flipping through TV channels.

"I wanted to mention that I'm bringing a friend with us, to the concert."

"What?" You are very alert now.

"She's a very special friend. And I've invited her to come with us to the show."

You can't believe what you have just heard.

"Dad, why do you have to bring someone? Tell her you have to cancel, so we can just go the two of us."

There is a long pause over the line.

"I can't do that. I promised her."

"You promised *me*, Dad." A cold feeling spreads over your body; you can feel your palms growing strangely clammy.

"We'll have fun honey. I can't change things around now. Just wait and see."

But you don't have to. The next morning you wake up with your throat swollen half shut, a fever, and red welts on your palms and the soles of your feet.

It's those mysterious welts that worry your mother. After your exam, the doctor announces "hand, foot, and mouth disease," which sounds worse than it is. Just a virus, but you will have to stay in bed.

So in the end, you never see George Michael.

You learn the secrets of your parents' marriage slowly, the truth unfolding to you like the disassembly of an intricate paper crane.

When you are eleven they tell you they are getting divorced. They call you into their room. Your brothers, the six-year-old annoyance and the baby, are somewhere else. Your mother pulls you onto their bed (now her bed) with the rainbow sheets. Your father stands by the closet. She wraps you in her arms, arms that once embraced him easily but lately, your foggy eleven-year-old mind seems to suspect, have been busy with a different man you think you've seen lurking around, maybe since all the way last year when your mom got pregnant with your baby brother. She will go on to embrace many men but never the right one.

What happens to all his records? They go away in boxes, a moving truck, a basement, you don't know where. You're not sure what happens to your own records.

When you are twenty-three, you drive all night down a long, dark coast. To your right is the wide ocean, to your left inky fields of garlic and artichoke. You are moving from San Francisco to the desert, from the cool breast of a state to the dry soles of its feet. You are on your own for the first time, though you have felt lonely, on and off, for years.

You have gone to school, gotten a degree like you are supposed to, written papers and mopped floors and made humdrum love to unremarkable men. But you have no idea what you are doing. Now it is time for your life to begin, and you are afraid of where you're going and what you will find. You are afraid you will find nothing at all.

To keep you company on the road, and awake, you spin the radio dial. Some station out of somewhere comes in, playing a song you remember but haven't heard for a long, long while.

A fine rain starts. You roll down the window, let the mist in and the music out. For a few minutes you are five again: thick pigtails, marrying Barbie to Ken, waking up early to sneak an episode of cartoons, slipping another record on your turntable.

How to Buy a Record

You grow up to marry an impossibly good man.

You first meet in the desert. He's your co-worker and invites you out to show you around town. You go to a lounge, buy ten-dollar martinis your new paycheck can't afford. When the live band from Los Angeles plays a Cuban jazzy set, he brushes past all the self-conscious scenesters in velvet banquettes and breaks down like a crazed chicken, long hair wild, arms flapping on the dance floor. You are still a bit afraid of life. But you laugh and laugh until your martini hurts in your stomach.

One night in your third year of marriage the two of you make love and then go to a concert, where you jump around in the heat and pulse and sweat for hours, getting lost in the thumping electronic sound and the sour drinks so you can forget the angst of the past eight months, of trying to get pregnant and failing.

While you dance on the sticky club floor like music is all that matters, inside you the right sperm is going to the right egg and your baby is being made.

Years later, for some reason you pretend is not overly nostalgic, you decide that a great birthday present for your five-year-old daughter, your youngest, would be her own record player. Forget a CD player, like her seven-year-old sister has. It's time to go old-school.

You go to eBay. You type in "children's vinyl records." A tidal wave of results hits you, a wistful shit-storm, a bludgeon. It turns out no one is making new vinyl albums for kids, though grownup vinyl is in the midst of a revival. You have to go vintage, sift through decades. You refine your search.

What you see: The cover images of actual records you owned (!).

What you really see: you at six, you in saddle shoes, you with a balloon tied around your wrist, you hugging a sand pail, on a sailboat, at the zoo with a peacock nipping your behind, flanked by your parents, haloed in yellow sunlight.

Some things you buy arrive in the mail. You set them aside for a couple of weeks. The birthday passes. The record player is received (your daughter is mildly interested) but most of the records remain in their packages. You worry if you open these records, time capsules hermetically sealed in their original sleeves, you will spring a leak you cannot stanch.

A few weeks later comes the annual fundraising auction for your daughters' school. The auctions are serious business—evening affairs held at fancy venues, attendance required if you want to stay in good social standing. The theme this year is: "Eighties! We Got The Beat."

You and your husband cobble together costumes with a sort of *Flashdance*-meets-*Pretty in Pink* theme. The night before the auction he pulls up an eighties mix online and you hold an impromptu family dance party in the living room. Your little girls wiggle until their curls plaster to their foreheads, trying on your musical childhood as though it's a new item from the nursery room dress-up bin.

This is it, you think as you watch them dance, *here are their lives, happening right now.*

Your husband does his flappy arms thing.

Weeks after the school auction, when no one is around, you finally tear open one of the envelopes from eBay.

Records still come out of the sleeve best with a soft shake into the right hand.

It's the same as you remember. The colors of the label are faded now, less vibrant than they once seemed. But the record still has survived, largely undamaged.

Lift the disc to your cheek. Close your eyes. You must do this with eyes closed, you're not sure why.

Rub the vinyl skin back and forth across your own.

The record player, the new one, sleek and silver and way too lightweight, is right here.

Feel the hole at the center of the record with your finger, ease the spindle through. A perfect coupling.

There's a switch for the arm, of course. Flick it. It lifts, travels over, descends.

· Natalie Singer ·

Wait.
The static.
Then … it goes …
Around, and around, and around.

PIECES OF ME
By Deli Moussavi-Bock

This weekend is the first time, after almost eleven years together, that my parents will meet Halley, my spouse, wife, partner, lover—whatever name one chooses to call two women who are married to each other. We are headed from our Seattle home, where we live together, to Long Beach for my cousin Reza's wedding. Some of my extended family—all first- or second-generation immigrants from Iran—will be there. It's hard for me to believe this day has come when Halley and my dad will be standing next to one another.

Seven or eight years have passed since my father sent a birthday card on my thirtieth birthday that read, "I hope you enjoy this picture. I wish you were never born." The card was a gorgeous photograph of a favorite spot for both of us. I could tell it was carefully chosen. The scene was a spotless azure sky in Pacific Grove, where we used to live. Chiseled cliffs overlooking the Monterey Bay are covered by small, springtime, purple flowers called Persian Carpets by locals. During fall semester off from college in 1991, this is where I had parked during lunch breaks from my two law internships. That was the semester when I found out I had no interest in the practical application of law. That was the semester I was fortunate to be home to call the ambulance when my mom had a minor stroke.

When Halley and I first arrive at Long Beach Airport, irritability comes in spurts. I worry about the tension the situation wedges between us.

"Did you get directions to the hotel?" she asks.

"No, I ran out of time. And, you didn't get full directions from the Alamo car lady while we were at Alamo," I say. We snip at each other in our rental car.

We have no idea when the first meeting with my parents will take place. It doesn't help that my cousin, Gelareh, called me a few minutes after we landed to remind me how volatile my father can be. She is a couple months older than me and moved to the US from Iran four years ago. She's a woman of backbone, having urged me to come out to *her* parents—evolved humans whom my mother and father look up to—while they visited from Iran. Gelareh is a good bridge between me and my father; she understands my generation and also understands what it's like to be raised in the Persian culture.

On the phone she says, "I just want to remind you to relax. We're not sure what your father will do. Even if he causes a scene, an outburst, you don't react. Just as you have a right to be upset by his reaction, by the way he was raised, he has the right to be uncomfortable and not understand your life."

"She has a point," I say to Halley. "He has the right not to understand. But why did she have to say 'even if he causes a scene'?"

My agitation grows. It's hard for me not to engage, to drop the armor and not defend myself when someone, particularly my father, attacks me. My mind flashes to a time a few years ago when Halley and I sat in Shahram and Maria's first rental house waiting to meet my parents, while my mother and father sat out front in their parked car, in the cold and dark, and refused to meet Halley.

I am resolved to put my best foot forward and *do* this. The stakes are high. This is Reza's and his fiancé's weekend. It's not about me and my family drama.

After many misturns driving, every guess I venture is wrong.

"*Make a U-turn here. Take a left. Sorry, I meant take a right. I said it backwards. There! Shit, okay, not there. Turn around,*" I say.

We finally turn into the hotel parking lot. In the lobby I greet my Aunt Mina, her husband, and then their son, Reza.

My aunt flings her arms around me. Uncle Hadi grasps Halley. Reza embraces us. First meeting down, I think to myself. Years ago, when I finally came out as gay to Aunt Mina and Uncle Hadi, ten years after our ceremony had taken place, they immediately sent us a wedding gift, a beautiful large crystal picture frame. They had no idea the ceremony had ever taken place. My parents had begged me to lie to my relatives about my 'situation.'

Halley and I unload luggage and head to Main Street in old town Seal Beach to grab dinner and relax before the inevitable meeting with my parents. On our way to the car, I'm stunned to see familiar faces. My mom and my sister-in-law, Maria, with two-year-old Peyton in her arms, are walking toward me. My dad and my brother, Shahram, are farther away, unloading the car around the corner. Our first instinct, Halley's and mine, is to jump into our car simply to make this moment easier on all of us. I remember how Shahram had told me that when my dad found out I was gay, he collapsed to the ground sobbing. As if I had died.

My mom spots me. Maria calls, "Oh my God, hi!"

"Mom, this is Halley. Halley this is my mom." I say. No time to think. All I can do is be present in the moment.

Halley smiles, her voice sincere, inviting, "Hi, it's so nice to meet you."

Her face is open, washed in soft dusk light. She's wearing a long, ankle-length, white summer skirt, a black tank top and black beaded sandals, red painted toes exposed.

My mom says an emphatic and slightly strained, "Hi" with her thick Farsi accent.

She hugs Halley instinctively, and I am impressed. I watch my dad linger back by the car, waiting for my brother to unload. He's hesitating, I know. After what seems like quite a while, he sees he's been spotted and walks toward us. I spring forward before he can say anything and say, "Dad, this is Halley, Halley this is my dad."

Halley reaches out her hand, and my dad's hand meets hers. His smile is tense, hers, framed by a tan and easy blonde hair, is protected.

Halley is five feet eleven, long-legged, with a pure child-joy smile. She is fair-skinned, with red, soft-rounded cheeks, golden-hazel eyes, and full, red lips. She is gorgeous, athletic, and humble, yet in stature she towers above my parents. My mom and dad are five feet and five feet three, respectively. My dad's wavy salt-and-pepper hair frames small, alarmingly sky-blue eyes. My mom's reddish-brown hair sweeps back from her face revealing illuminated brown eyes and full lips. She is a beautiful woman with very little self-confidence. They're like love birds, my parents. My dad calls her "Beauty". He adores her as much as I adore Halley.

The first meeting has taken place, by accident, everyone caught off guard. I thank my angels for this.

We have all been brought together by Reza's wedding.

After the impromptu meeting in the parking lot, I'm touched that my mom makes sure we're included in everything. She's come a long way from the phone calls that would invariably end in how she thought this gay thing was a passing phase. An eleven-year phase?

It seems to me that Shahram and my parents stick together. Often on trips my parents take, Shahram and his family follow. I felt a pang inside me when they all flew to Germany to visit my aunt and uncle and then to Paris. I'd always wanted to go to Paris, especially with my mom. I was invited, but Halley wasn't. For years I have repeatedly been invited to my family gatherings with one condition: that I come alone. Thanksgiving, Christmas, my brother's wedding. I've declined most of them. Though deeply upset, I attended Shahram and Maria's wedding alone, pretending to be single.

My mom invites Halley and me to dinner, and again to lunch the next day. We all end up staying on the same floor at the hotel. As the weekend progresses, it seems dreamlike that we are pulled gently closer and closer into the heart of the family. At dinner, on our first night together, we are seated at two separate booths—all that was available. My parents sit with my aunt and uncle. My brother, his wife and kids, and Halley and I sit together. We wave to my parents every now and then. I'm relieved of the pressure to engage in conversation.

But the next day at lunch we are all seated together. Halley and I talk with my father over lunch.

"Now, how many siblings do you have?" Halley asks my father.

"Nine," he says. He's animated now, although a moment before he was reserved, avoiding eye contact with Halley. He's flattered by her genuine questions about his life. "I have nine brothers and sisters."

"Which number are you?" Halley asks. Her curiosity about him draws him in.

"I'm the third oldest," my dad says, glancing at me. I can't believe he's engaging with Halley, and he sees my surprise, joy, and hope that this will last.

I'm surprised at his response. What? Third oldest? My paternal grandma Fakhri, my dad would tell me, used to urge her husband to take my dad on errands because it got rid of eighty-five percent of the naughtiness she had to deal with from her kids. I was always certain my dad was third *youngest*.

"Yes, I was the third oldest." He smiles, relishing this talk about his childhood.

"Dad, I thought you were the third youngest because you were so naughty."

He turns to Halley, "When I was a child, before we had refrigerators my mom used to prepare food and lock it in a chest until meal time so we kids wouldn't eat it before dinner or lunch." He tells Halley how he would pick the lock, eat skewers of kabobs, and sell some to his siblings.

"Wow, what an entrepreneur!" Halley says.

My father laughs and takes this compliment in.

In 1975 when I was five, my father moved our family to Palo Alto from Iran. He'd won a scholarship at Stanford for graduate work in education. After a few years in the US, the Iranian Revolution changed our fate, and we never moved back to Iran. My father's rose garden in the front yard of our house in Rasht, Iran is one of the things I remember most about Iran.

When I was thirteen, I had dreams in which I flew to Iran before dawn, unseen, across the lush valleys of Gilan, across deserts. I flew in the open air, past oil fields, over rice fields with my body. No need for a plane.

Not more than a couple of years after our move from Iran, when we thought we'd return someday to Kooyeh Bayani, my father's routine was to take me on errands in our brown Toyota Celica. During our drives, he'd recite Persian poetry: Hafiz, Qhayam, Saadi. Most often he would recite Saadi. One of Saadi's poems was about how twelve million people died over a myth. Poems about the human condition. He recites the words with heart, how humans killed each other for stories. I'd feel his love of these ancient words. He encouraged me to write poems when I was six years old.

"When you grow up, you can work for the United Nations. A humanitarian is what you want to be. Follow your passion, because you can only be successful by following your heart."

Years later when I was in my thirties, when my dad and I argued about gays and history, I had repeated Halley's words to him: "History has shown us that there's always some group of people we want to hold down to make ourselves feel better. Gays are one of them right now. Iranians were in the '70s. You never know who it'll be next."

At the hotel, after lunch at the Macaroni Grill and before the rehearsal dinner at a Persian restaurant, Halley and I find myself in my parents' suite, my dad with shaving cream on his face, helping my mom decide what to wear. "Mitty, that's fine, wear that."

Pretty soon everyone is in the room, aunt, uncle. Everyone talks over each other, as usual. "Hurry up and shave." "Where did you put my cologne?" "I don't know, do these shoes match?"

My mom then gives me a gift, a beautiful Coach satin cocktail purse. She gives Halley a gift, an attractive and practical black, cross-body Coach purse. She's been giving me birthday gifts for years. Halley's birthday has always passed unacknowledged.

As we leave the room, Halley says, "That was so sweet. Your mother reached out her hand to my cheek, pulled me close and kissed my cheek."

At the rehearsal dinner later that night, Halley and I take our seats at a long table next to my family. She sits next to my mother and they talk throughout the night. I think about intervening to "manage" the conversation, but I realize they're fine on their own. Two adults in conversation.

The next day the wedding takes place in a beautiful Japanese garden. Reza finds us as Halley and I enter. He takes us to special seats he reserved for us and my brother and his family. The sun is bold, shining down on us. Green orchids adorn the bridesmaids' hair. A luscious green that ties everything together: the garden, the nature, the beauty of this day. It reminds me of our own ceremony—smaller and with none of my family present, long before same-sex marriage was legal in California.

· *We Came Back to Say* ·

We're about to head to the reception after the ceremony, when Reza yells, "the Moussavi family, please gather here for pictures. Moussavis, come!"

Halley is talking to one of the bridesmaids. The rest of us are lined up: Reza, his bride, Lauren, my mom, dad, Shahram, Maria, Mina, Hadi, his sisters. Halley hangs back. Reza looks at her and yells, "Hello!? I said the Moussavis, here please." Halley rushes over. She completes the picture.

At the reception, I relish seeing my mom and my aunt twist to "Twist and Shout." Reza has taken all generations into consideration with his music mix. We laugh as my aunt gets down to "Baby Got Back" along with Reza's college friends. Guests pour onto the dance floor. We Persians teach the Americans how to dance Iranian-style. As we walk back to our table, Maria stops me and says, "We really missed out by not having Halley at our wedding." I thank her for this.

We toast our family members in Iran. My cousin, Gelareh, called her mom that night to tell her it was just like old times, all of us together. And now Halley's a part of it, pulled in tight. After the wedding, I call my grandma in Iran. She hasn't seen Peyton yet and hasn't met Reza's fiancé or Halley. Energized, she swears to me that same night she had a dream we all got together and she was there. She *was* there.

A few months after the wedding, I fly to my parents' home in Monterey to surprise visiting aunts, Gelareh, my brother and his family—an amazing time of Iranian feasting, toasts, and jokes. When it comes time to leave, it dawns on me that my family is reassembling. It's been a long time coming and now that it's here, it feels so easy yet so stunning. I am present to what I feel. The Ganges dammed flood of emotions threatens to rip my throat apart. I only let my eyes water.

We caravan to the airport. I ride with my dad and my mom. We get out of the car. My father walks ahead of the rest of the family with me.

He holds my elbow, tells me in Farsi, "*Bebeen, dokhtareh man.* Look, my daughter…I love you more than the world."

It's one of the most sincere moments of conversation we've had. He sees me. I am present. I let myself receive his love.

FRENCH MAIDS

By Paul Boardman

I FOUND MYSELF IN THE ARMS OF A WOMAN, my very first woman, after one of my early grave disappointments as a teen. I was seventeen years old. It was 1975, at the end of cross country season.

The Far East Cross Country championships were held at Tama Retreat Center outside of Tokyo. Our rag-tag team of missionary kids took a lot of pride in outrunning the huge US military schools and all the expat schools, where the kids were cooler, sported much fancier uniforms, and wore more expensive running shoes. But we missionary kids ran them down on the hills, because we were better trained, because we were taught to run for God's glory. We didn't know exactly what that meant, but we believed there was some grand purpose to everything we did, even the little things. We prayed before every meet, in a circle, touching hands, heads down, earnest, fervent, presenting a spectacle to the other teams who would slip in a jab at us when we were toeing the start line. "Holy rollers!" they would mock us before the gun went off.

The cross country course was run through an old Japanese military encampment that the American army had taken over during the Occupation at the end of WWII. The US Army still maintained it as a retreat center. Rumor had it that, as the Occupation was being imposed in the late 1940s, the earth in the encampment was poisoned by the defeated departing Japanese army, and that there was still undetonated ordinance on the grounds. We made sure we didn't wander into the woods too far when we went for a pre-race-jitters pee. Bordering the course were concrete bunkers and pillboxes with gun slits. All these wartime reminders lent to us runners the aura of competing on a battleground; there was a lot at stake.

I had won every meet during the regular season, but the Far East Championship was different. At the Championship there were teams from the Philippines, Korea, Okinawa, Hong Kong. Every international school in the Far East was invited. The start line stretched a long way across and many boys deep. There were rumors that Saul Hardeman, from the Philippines, was the best runner in Asia. He was also undefeated. Like me, he was a missionary kid. Like our team, his Faith Academy team, a Christian boarding school in Manila, bowed their heads and laid their hands on top of one another's, praying to God that whatever happened on this day would reflect and showcase His Glory.

When the gun went off I knew I had to get out ahead of the mayhem of the hundreds of bodies jockeying for position. I found myself pinned behind a phalanx of runners from Okinawa. Ahead I could see the tiny Saul scampering away. I pulled wide and ran in the woods to get around the Okinawa team that was blocking my way. I came up behind Saul, letting him feel my tall presence but choosing not to challenge him. I was going to wait for Gut Hill to make my surge and demoralize him.

We ran steady for a spell. When we reached Gut Hill, that long stretch of steep grade that broke many a runner, I let him face it, look up the steep long road as I slightly accelerated with a lean into the hill and passed him. He hung behind me clinging to my pace. At the top, we were both winded but we faced a downhill stretch, a chance to recover. As we bounded down and passed through the halfway mark of the loop of cheering spectators, we were neck and neck.

I had never run at such a pace at any of the previous meets. We were both being aggressive, and I was worried that I wouldn't be able to sustain the pace for the last loop. We jousted with each other for the entire course, and coming up to Gut Hill for the second time again I tried to surge, knowing I didn't have much left, but he stayed with me. As we crested and headed into the downhill he seemed to fast forward, reaching for every reserve. I tried to stay with him, but as we entered the clearing at the finish line he accelerated several paces ahead of me. When I crossed the finish line in second place, I felt so disappointed that I had to fight off the embarrassment of tears. I should have done something differently. I couldn't see how second place gave anyone, much less God, any glory at all.

On the team bus back to school I sat next to Caleb, who reassured me that as long as I had done my best that was all that was required.

"I mean really, Paul, second place in the Far East is amazing. But I have an idea," Caleb said with a grin.

"What's your idea?" I asked sullenly.

"You can stay at my house tonight. We will take the train to Tokiwadai and go to a bar near the station. I pass it every day on my way home from school. It looks like a club; in front there are sandwich-board signs with pictures of pretty Japanese women dressed in French maid costumes. You can sit with them and drink a beer for Yen 1000. It's expensive but worth it to be able to be around these pretty women. They will cheer you up."

Caleb sounded so sure of himself, like he had been planning this for some time. Bringing me along gave him the courage he needed to venture inside.

After the bus arrived we showered, and took the train to Ikebukuro, then one more train to Tokiwadai. As foreigners, standing in front of this "French Maid Bar," we caught the curious stares of Japanese passing by. We wondered if we should really go in.

We counted the money in our wallets to make sure we each had our Yen 1000 for the one beer we were going to drink. We had more than enough. Maybe even enough for two drinks. We were going to blow the wad. The posters of the Japanese women in maid costumes looked cheery and sexy. I was nervous there, at the threshold of the bar; I had never done anything like this before, never inserted myself so blatantly into a place I didn't rightly belong. But it seemed fun to give it a try. So Caleb led the way down the stairs and through a gaudy gold door.

Just inside the entrance, a young guy in a black suit, obviously the manager, asked us some questions. He was hesitant at first to let us in. I could tell he didn't know our ages. I was six-foot-five and Caleb was six-foot-one, taller than almost any Japanese. He made sure that we spoke Japanese. Age didn't seem to be his concern. When he determined that we spoke Japanese, he led us to a table.

Immediately, two women dressed in short maid costumes came over, sat beside us, and pressed themselves up tightly against us. They wore black stockings, but their maid skirts were so short that we could see the white flesh of their soft thighs where the garters connected to their stockings. Their French maid collars were scooped down low to show white, powdered cleavage.

The women asked us what we wanted to drink.

"Beer, please," We answered politely.

They put in orders for beers for themselves, too. It seemed like a party was starting to happen. They seemed interested in us, the foreigners. They giggled and gestured warmly, not seeming to question that we were twenty-two, the lie that we had concocted. We were outsiders, so they seemed to think that we were outside the rules.

I was beginning to forget about the day's humiliating defeat. As we all raised our glasses for a "cheers", the woman sitting next to me, Momoko, put her hand high up on my thigh and squeezed. She put her arm on my shoulder and grabbed a fistful of my hair at the nape. I was taken by surprise, but I liked it: it felt good.

Caleb said, interjecting with a grin, in English, "So is your woman putting her hand on your thigh?"

"Yes, she is," I replied, nonchalantly.

He raised his glass again, smiling "Here's to French women's hands on our thighs!" The women again raised their glasses and twittered. Caleb and I thought it funny that they didn't know what they had just toasted to. It seemed sexy.

Momoko was about thirty years old. She had on a lot of makeup but I conjured her to be beautiful. I decided that she was, even if I suspected that she wasn't exactly a natural beauty. She smiled a lot and spoke in a very high tone, a falsetto. She gazed into my eyes as she spoke, continuing to stroke my neck and rub my thigh. But her caresses were quickly becoming so much more intimate that I began to feel faint twinges of guilt beneath my heady excitement. All the while she cooed at me, smiling and laughing as if it was the most perfectly normal thing in the world to be so intimately touching a stranger. I wanted to abandon myself to the illicit excitement of the place, of Momoko, and her revealing costume, but at the same time it seemed preposterous. I found myself lost in a world so far removed from my normal grind of school, chapel, training and racing, that I wondered if it might just be some sort of hallucinogenic dream from which I would soon awaken. Before my beer was finished she was touching me in a way I had never been touched by a woman before.

Caleb piped up, "Is she doing to you…you know…what this woman is doing to me?"

"Yes, she is," I said weakly.

Caleb replied, echoing my wonderment before fading back into his revelry, "Isn't this just crazy?"

When another French maid walked by, Momoko called her over to join in the fun. All three women giggled and laughed as they fondled us. It all seemed so light-hearted, still in the frivolous spirit of a party. I had always expected—because this is what we had been taught—that my first sexual experience would be with The Woman provided by God, and that the event would be serious, quiet, momentous and private.

But here it all was, my desire and sexuality on public display. It seemed very wrong, but also somewhat right. I was confused. Like something this easy, this animalistic or fleshly, couldn't be *all* bad. It didn't feel quite sordid; not as bad as it should have felt. It felt irresistibly exciting.

Momoko grabbed my hand when a song she liked came on. She wanted me to dance with her. In my seventeen years I had never danced, but I wanted to humor my girl. I got up and immediately stayed close to her, not wanting to show my excitement to the whole club. She was tiny, coming up only to below my chest. She lead our slow-dance, continuing to touch me dreamily.

Caleb and his woman were on the dance floor now, too. He had his eyes closed, like he just wanted this moment to endure but also maybe to escalate, to reach some ultimate, fulfilling end. We lolled by each other, in a strange awkward waltz, each lost in the arms of our French maids.

After a time we returned to our table and our entire table slipped into animal silence. The lights had been turned down. The music was still playing. Caleb and I ordered another beer. Momoko leaned into me and embraced me. She continued to stroke my hair and neck. We finished our second beer, still heavily making out. We knew that we did not have money for a third. But the women became insistent on us ordering another. We resisted their pleas and declined. The manager came and kneeled in front of Momoko and whispered something. Momoko got up to go with him somewhere, disappearing. I went to the bathroom. When I came back Caleb was still embracing his woman. The woman was still, gently, trying to get him to order another beer.

I sat down, waiting for Momoko, excited to return to the intimacy she offered, the warmth of her embrace. But when I looked around the bar, I was surprised to see her seated across the room, at a table of other Japanese men. I looked quickly away, trying not to feel abandonment or hurt. I didn't know what love was, but I felt myself to be in love with her. I thought she liked me, that she had chosen me to spend her time and affection on. I felt we had a connection.

"We should pay and go," I said quickly to Caleb. He could see that Momoko had left.

"Where did she go?" he asked.

"She is sitting over there with some other men," I replied morosely, feeling strangely hurt. "I think it's time to leave."

He told his woman that we were ready for the bill. We got up to go. Caleb went to the bathroom while I moved toward the entrance. I made certain not to look at Momoko with her other men.

As I waited for Caleb, the manager came and offered the bill to me with two hands and a slight bow, like he was apologizing in advance to me to be handing to me this impending trouble. I looked down and thought for a moment that I had misread the number of zeroes. It read 2,000 Yen, I first thought, less than we were expecting to pay. Perhaps they missed the second beers? I wondered.

But as I looked again I saw with a sinking heart that it actually read 20,000 Yen, ten times the amount of two beers.

Caleb came out and I shoved the bill into his hand, saying as calmly as I could, "They say we owe them 20,000 Yen. I don't see how that is remotely possible."

Caleb looked at the bill and seemed stunned.

"What are we going to do? We have nothing near that," he said.

"I have no idea. Maybe we can come back and pay more later."

Caleb looked at me, his jaw clenched. After a pause, he said, "I think we should make a run for it. Just sprint out of here."

I asked, in as non-inflected a voice as possible, like we were just discussing the weather in English, "What do you mean, like literally run away and not pay the bill?"

By now the host, standing by watching our discussion, seemed puzzled, perhaps guessing that there might be trouble collecting his money. He kept a professional smile on as we were discussing this in English in front of him. But we knew he couldn't understand a word we said.

"Yes," Caleb said, firmly, with determination. "When I say 'thigh' we will both bolt up the stairs and dash toward my house. Are you in?"

"OK, I'm in," I replied, trying fast to summon my courage.

I clutched my gym bag. Caleb paused for a second, handed the bill back to the host and reached for his back pocket like he was going to pull out his wallet to pay. Then suddenly he yelled "thigh!"

I reached for the door, slammed it open, and we flew up the stairs. The host yelled after us to wait, "Matte!"

He had been startled enough that we had a head start, but he ran after us, full of indignation. He was halfway up the stairs when we had reached the top stair. On the street, we turned right, nearly crashing into two Japanese salarimen. We bounded down the street, headed toward the residential area. The manager was still sprinting after us, cursing at us, calling other Japanese pedestrians to stop us.

But we ran hard, our second race of the day. We were larger than the Japanese. We were propelled forward by our youthful energy and the mortified panic of our wrong-doing. We turned a couple of corners and seemed to have lost him, but he rounded the turn and kept charging at us. I looked back and when I saw him, angry and determined to catch us, I yelled encouragement to Caleb, who seemed to be flagging, "He's sprinting! Faster!"

We surged on adrenaline. The distance between us and the manager increased. We ran up to a row of tightly walled houses. It was dark, and the street lights were dim. Our cross-country training seeming to be paying off. We began to gain, putting a safe distance between us and him. Panting, sweating, we turned another corner, furtively opened the front gate of a random stranger's house, closed it behind us and crumpled in exhaustion among the bonsai.

Slumped against the wall in the inner courtyard of a quiet Japanese house, we tried with all our might not to breathe. We refrained from talking. We tried to be as still as possible. We stayed put, pressed against each other, huddled, our backs against the moist winter wall.

· *We Came Back to Say* ·

Next to him, I could feel Caleb's heart pound inside his body. We sat like that, half propped up, half prone and frozen, against that cold Tokiwadai courtyard wall, willing ourselves into complete silence. We heard footsteps go by. We waited. We laid still. We stayed in the same position for over an hour, until all our muscles were sore and cramped. Our legs were stiff from the damp ground and all the tension. When we finally felt that the danger of being caught had passed, we stretched out and relaxed a little.

Caleb asked me solemnly, "So is this the worst thing you have ever done in your life?"

"Yeah, I am certain it is."

I asked him the same thing.

"Well, yeah probably so, but I have been to Ikebukuro porn theaters before. This is probably worse, though, right?"

"It's really bad," I replied. "I'm sure of that. Nothing about it serves God's glory."

But even as I confessed my guilt, I was troubled by the certainty that it had felt good. I knew I had somehow crossed over briefly into a nether world, one about which I knew nothing. Yet it was strange to me that this unfamiliar world existed so very close to my own.

CHEMISTRY

By Jeanne Verville

As a divorced woman of a certain age, dating just hasn't worked out that well for me. I've gone on many dates in the last twenty-five years and am still single. One of the problems might be that I'm a lawyer: some men seem intimidated by that. I've tried to flirt away the Lois Lane smart-as-nails assumption, hoping my dates will get that what I want is a man skilled at pulling out the girl in me who likes to laugh and have fun. Other men seem to want me to play the Nancy Reagan role of "admire and adore from the sidelines," but I'm no longer suited for it. And then there's me: I'm afraid of making a mistake and being hurt again. I want that chemistry that pushes me to override my fears and objections and tells me this guy is *right*.

I thought I'd found one man who at least seemed confident enough to try me. Andrew was smart, not yet old at sixty-seven, acceptably trim, decent looking, and successful in business. Many women would have jumped at the opportunity to win this serious, recent widower—invited him over for gourmet meals and the good conversation he said he enjoyed so much. Maybe they would have faked enthusiasm for his wooden kisses in exchange for the lifestyle he could provide. On paper, he looked good enough for me to keep seeing for eight months. *Maybe he's still in mourning and will change*, my head kept saying. Finally, I listened to my gut: *no fun, no chemistry, not for you*.

Now, after a year of feeling hopeless and wondering if I should settle for someone who doesn't excite me, I find that my recently acquired forty-two-year-old handyman has given a kick-ass jolt to my libido. At sixty-eight, I'd thought it was dead. Suddenly I'm walking around with, like, a permanent hard-on. I fantasize about taking him to my tousled bed of persimmon-colored sheets. I see him hovering over me, his breath on my face, his perfect, plump lips nearing mine. I see him kissing me, softly at first, teasingly, then urgently. I imagine him deep inside me and long, shuddering contractions releasing the exquisite pain I've carried now for weeks. The message is unexpected but ever so welcome: my hormones are still active. I want to have sex!

When Chad first showed up at my door wearing a good, charcoal sweater I felt my breath catch. Such wide shoulders and so handsome in that tall, dark way I've always favored. He's been here on and off now for two months, and the repairs have morphed into his painting the kitchen and the bathroom and staining the deck. I'm running out of money but keep asking him back, trying to figure out a way to seduce him. Before I was a lawyer, I was bold: "You want dessert first, or me?" Now, I'm afraid to ask for what I want. All these years of living in my head as a lawyer—analyzing, finding flaws, arguing—doing a man's job, in 1960s parlance— have made me distrust my feminine desirability.

The last time my burners fired so hot was, I hate to admit, twenty-four years ago, right after law school but before I dove into the competitive male arena of corporate America. I'd moved to a rented house in Seattle's Mountlake area. My children remained in the Midwest with my ex-husband for the six weeks I needed to study for the bar exam. My former law-school lover, Dean, was in Seattle studying for the bar too, and we agreed he could rent a room in the house. He'd told me two weeks earlier he was in love with a woman in Idaho he planned to marry.

But his words had fallen on deaf ears. Before he arrived, I'd been filled with fantasy: we would spend the days studying, the nights making love. He'd been such a wonderful lover for the year we were together, before he transferred to another university. We were mutually attracted on the first day of law school, where I'd found myself at age forty-one after a brutal divorce, but it had taken a few months to work up the nerve enough to shed my1950s "good-girl" repressions and ask him to be my lover. An insightful, handsome man eighteen years my junior with a beautiful baritone voice, Dean had big, slow hands and took care that I was happy. He made me laugh and feel beautiful and helped heal the sting of divorce. And he smiled when we made love, something new in my limited experience.

The first night after Dean moved in to the Mountlake house was spent studying on different floors. At around 11 o'clock I went upstairs to him and put my hands on his shoulders.

"Why don't you take a break now? It's late," I said. "I'm ready for bed."

He stood and, after stretching his six-two frame, turned to me, "Jeanne, we're not going to have sex. I'm in love with Danielle. I'm going to be true to her."

I retreated downstairs to my bed of flowered sheets, feeling rejected and embarrassed. But I couldn't sleep. My entire body ached with desire for him. I wanted to go to that lovely place he showed me where time slows and the mind takes a back seat to feeling. Enough with the mind. Mine wanted a break.

I had never experienced physically *painful* desire for my husband Dieter in the nineteen years I'd known him. I enjoyed sex and we were experimental; he tried to please me up to a point but, in the end, it was really all about him, in and out of bed. After a couple of times with Dean, I felt like Geena Davis did after her fling with Brad Pitt in *Thelma and Louise*. His soft and gentle patience awakened a sexuality my husband had never fully ignited. With him, I relaxed into a state of trust and pleasure, in which I didn't feel I *had* to perform or please. His smile told me all I needed to know.

My fantasy with Dean that summer wasn't to be. Nor would it be with anyone else, as my femininity and passion were soon dampened by the demands of a lawyer's life—a fast-paced life lived entirely in the head, amid competitive, married men. I zipped my inclination to flirt and stuffed my emotions, as I concentrated on becoming assertive, authoritative, and articulate. I could not afford to be vulnerable and soft. My mind was to be my tool of survival.

Before that tearful night when Dean rejected me twenty-four years ago and now with Chad, the only other time I'd experienced a truly painful flush of sexual desire was in France, just before my marriage ended. My husband was attending a scientific conference at an elegant old resort hotel on the beach in Brittany. I hoped the week together, without the children and in this romantic setting, might revive a love I hadn't fully acknowledged was too dead to be resuscitated for even one night. I tried to seduce him, but he wouldn't touch me. I was perplexed, not realizing then that he was having an affair.

A Belgian scientist named Dom befriended us in his role as one of the conference organizers. He had an unorthodox appearance and wore drab scientist/nerd clothes. He was tall and gawky, like an Ichabod Crane, but had beautiful green eyes and was charming, gracious, and welcoming. Over the week, we became pals. He introduced me to ruby-colored kir cocktails and snifters of headily fragrant amber calvados. One day at the beach, we found ourselves lying next to each other on striped beach towels, gazing deeply into each other's eyes. His gaze seemed to penetrate my soul. He was interested in what I had to say. He made me laugh. The way he looked at me made me feel beautiful. At the dance on the final night of the conference, he swirled me around the dance floor, literally sweeping me off my feet in his mastery of the Viennese waltz. He made me feel alive—and dizzy.

At the end of the conference, Dieter and I went to Paris, where we spent the night with Dom and his wife in their elegant Paris apartment with high ceilings and French doors. After dinner, I offered to tidy up the kitchen. As I stood finishing the dishes, Dom came into the room. We were alone. "Thank you. You really didn't have to do this."

"I wanted to," I said, looking into the murky dishwater.

Suddenly he was behind me, his arms around me, holding me close. I was surprised but did not resist; nor did I turn and try to make more of it. We were both married. But I felt a surprising flush engulf my being. The unbearable heat was one I had never experienced, sadly, in my entire forty years. That night, I lay awake for hours.

The next day, Dieter took a train to Berlin and I accidentally missed mine to Copenhagen, with no other trains leaving until the next day. I felt a profound sense of sadness and an aching loneliness as I wandered around the Left Bank. Warm tears streamed behind my dark glasses as I leaned over the railing on *Île de la Cité,* staring into the inky waters of the Seine.

I made a bold decision. I called Dom at work.

"Dom, I missed my train. Will you come and spend the day with me?" I asked in a halting voice, husky with tears. If he said 'yes,' I was prepared to go to a hotel and make love, marriages be damned.

"Jeanne, I can't do that. I'm at work. And you know we're both married."

I felt rejected. But all was not lost. After sixteen years in a dead marriage, the universe had sent me what I needed most: affirmation that I was still a desirable woman. This affirmation no doubt fueled my innate passion for life, driving me to evolve and leave the marriage just a year later.

Back to the present. Yesterday I saw Chad, the painter/handyman, standing at the door to my bedroom, his hand above his head on the door frame, looking at the folds of persimmon linens. And I wondered, was he thinking what it would be like to take me there?

Was he thinking of me at all? He's flirted with me, tickled my irreverent sense of humor. We've eaten lunch together six times at my table. He's shared his Tom Waits CDs, given me CDs he's cut of his own music. I've obsessed on a line on the CD of his love songs that goes, "You're beautiful in my eyes." I want to be beautiful in someone's eyes again.

But I don't sense a desire on his part to seduce me, which really doesn't surprise me. He's probably leery of me, the educated lawyer, and the master in this working relationship. And the age factor is real this time. While Dean had been eighteen years younger when I was in my early forties, Chad is twenty-six years younger. Demi Moore and other *younger* cougars notwithstanding, I know my fantasy with him is completely unrealistic. But I don't consider age a deterrent in the larger, general scheme. I will not be deterred in my search for a man who loves me as I am and sparks chemistry and passion.

I'm grateful Chad came into my life. He appeared just as I was rediscovering the gentleness of real life after semi-retiring from the competitive corporate world. I don't think he "gets" me at all and probably doesn't have the insight or background to do so. But he's touched me. By happily fixing all the things on my to-do list, he's lightened my burden of total self-sufficiency. He's made me feel taken care of. For years, I've worn my independence like a shield; now I find I'm ready to let someone be kind to me.

Chad has served as a catalyst in my recovery from years of being engulfed in my own male energy that fueled my survival. He's made me feel sexy. Now, instead of wearing suits, I've started showing a little cleavage and am choosing tight jeans again. Instead of a short, professional hairdo, I've let my hair grow and have highlights for the first time. Instead of applying the full mask of makeup, I'm trying a softer, more natural look.

Chad's presence has ignited a joyous passion for life and has lit my creative spark. I'm listening to more music that makes me *move*, and I'm even writing poetry. I've regained an interest in cooking and growing flowers, which tells me I'm reclaiming my femininity.

Everywhere I go, men are giving me a second look and I'm smiling and flirting. I love this new sexual energy so much I feel ready to let go of fear and try for the real thing. So I'm getting out on the golf course, on the water, and on the stream bank with a fly rod in hand—where the men are. It won't be Chad, but I feel confident that someone right is going to join me in my soft persimmon nest very soon.

BEARING MAX

By Wendy Staley Colbert

During the last trimester of my pregnancy, both the prospect of my baby's disability and the prospect of his death frightened me. From the time I was seven months pregnant, I knew he wasn't expected to live long. I wasn't sure I was up to being his mother. I wasn't sure I could handle the pain. I wasn't sure I could love him enough and then let him go.

The ultrasound technician picked up anomalies during the second trimester in a routine exam, pressing the wand against my slippery, swollen belly over and over to get a detailed look at his abnormal kidneys. Kidney defects are quite common and treatable, so we hoped for the best. Additional abnormalities showed up as my pregnancy progressed. Subsequent scans showed six toes on each foot and an extra flap of a digit on each hand. An amniocentesis early in my seventh month provided the damning diagnosis. I took the call from Rebecca, the hospital's genetic counselor, around 6:00 pm on Friday, June 18th, my fifth wedding anniversary.

"Your son has Trisomy 13. Trisomy 13 babies don't live long. Each of the cells in his body carries an extra thirteenth chromosome. He will be severely developmentally disabled. He will never walk, talk, or feed himself."

I sobbed as Rebecca told me she'd leave a packet of information for us outside her office door. My husband, Mark, canceled our celebratory dinner reservations and picked up the manila envelope instead. Shocked, I sat down beside Mark on the couch and we flipped through the brochures together, beginning to realize the hopelessness of our son's condition even as we felt his kicks through my cotton, floral maternity dress.

I went to my baby shower the next day, and made the hard decision to keep the news and my feelings to myself a little longer. I wasn't yet ready to reveal this shift in our world. I choked back tears and smiled wanly as I opened pale blue terry cloth onesies and the stackable blocks I knew my son would never use.

We met with Rebecca the following week, and she reiterated what we had learned from the pamphlets—that Trisomy 13 is a random genetic mutation that occurs only once in 5,000 newborns. Many Trisomy 13 fetuses are miscarried. Most infants born with the syndrome die within the first three months of life.

Hearing Rebecca confirm these grim details felt like a body blow to my gut. I was seven and a half months along now and completely lost my appetite. I had to force myself to continue eating healthy foods. I bitterly thought, *So much for skipping coffee during my pregnancy. A lot of good that did.* The impact of caffeine on my baby's deformed body seemed absurd, but I kept up my nutritional discipline anyhow.

Rebecca had informed us that if we wanted to investigate ending the pregnancy, we could take our case to the hospital ethics board. My husband and I were glad this option was available, but decided we would prefer to let nature take its course. We didn't want the potential burden of guilt from the choice of such a late-term abortion in addition to our already-palpable grief and my growing fear. I worried that the baby would die inside me, and was reassured each time I felt him kick. Even worse, I worried that I wouldn't know how to care for a disabled baby, that I wouldn't be able to love a disabled baby enough.

I dealt with my fear by speaking with other mothers. A woman with whom I'd worked had carried a severely disabled baby to term only to see him stillborn. When I phoned her for advice on my situation, she told me, "Be prepared that your baby may not look like a normal baby." She also gave me a reference for the local funeral home she had used that provided free cremations for infants.

I spoke to the mother of a Trisomy 13 child in Eastern Washington whose son was still kept alive by a feeding tube. She told me that despite the hardships in the years since he'd been born, her son was the light of her life. She offered to stop by for a visit in the coming weeks so I could meet her son. Now eight months pregnant, I declined—I was afraid of how I'd react when I met her son. I thought I would break down crying upon meeting him and seeing the severity of his disability and felt ashamed that I might not be able to welcome her son as she so joyfully and admirably had.

A few days passed, and then my water suddenly broke as I stood up to leave work one afternoon, three-and-a-half weeks before my due date. I stopped in the office restroom to be sure, then drove myself home. My heart beat quickly as I threw a nightie and some preemie baby clothes into an overnight bag and called Mark.

"We have to miss our labor class tonight," I said.

"How come?" he asked.

"We're going to have the baby instead!"

On the drive to the hospital, I felt relieved that my son had beat the odds so far—he had survived the pregnancy, and I hadn't had to face him dying inside of me. I began to feel excited to meet this little fighter who apparently wanted life so badly. I also still felt scared—and was still not sure if I could love him if he didn't look "normal," and not sure I had the courage to be the mother he needed.

I labored for hours (painlessly, thanks to the epidural), and as my baby's head was crowning, my ob/gyn said, "I'm sorry—it doesn't look good—I don't think he made it." I sobbed as I continued pushing.

My son was born. I heard his strong cry and cried for joy myself. The doctor apologized—our son's scalp wasn't fully closed and had an open wound on it, and she had assumed as his head was crowning that he was dead.

We named him Max James. He had no sucking reflex and had difficulty swallowing; it was as if his body was telling him he wasn't meant to last on this earth. His eyes never opened. He had extra digits on his feet and hands, and numerous other physical and mental defects we couldn't see. But I was relieved to find him beautiful and felt a rush of love for him, smoothing the wisps of fine hair behind his ears as I held him. He was tough all right—he squirmed and stuck his chin out, his legs kicking, his fingers clenched into fists. He was unable to breastfeed, so a nurse showed my husband how to finger-feed him, dropping little drips of pumped breast milk from a tube attached to his finger into Max's mouth.

When we got ready to take him home the next day, one of the nurses leaned in the backseat of the car where I was strapping five-and-a-half-pound Max into the car seat and said, "Now, you enjoy every minute with him, won't you?" Tears pricked my eyes, and I swallowed a lump in my throat, realizing again that Max's time with us might be short.

My original fear of not being able to love Max turned into a fear of him dying. I was conflicted: I didn't want him to die, but I also didn't want him to live a life of such limited quality. I was afraid I wouldn't be able to handle the grief, that I wasn't up to the task.

At home, we held Max constantly. He even slept between Mark and me in our king-sized bed. As we were drifting off to sleep our first night home, Max's breathing became congested and raspy. We could hear fluid in his lungs. My husband took Max into the bathroom and clapped him on the back until gobs of green mucus landed in the white basin.

Over the next couple of days, we had a routine follow-up visit with a nurse who was alarmed that Max was extremely jaundiced and his weight had dropped nearly a pound. She instructed us to force-feed Max formula with a bottle and sent a nurse to our home to set Max up with a bili light blanket to help treat the jaundice. Max aspirated formula while the nurse was in our home, and before we knew it, she had resuscitated him and called 9-1-1. We were back in the hospital. The ER doctors told us they couldn't get all the fluid out of his lungs and Max's time was limited. We took him home, where our extended family met us and took turns holding Max, then left Mark and me for the evening.

Mark put *Kind of Blue*, his favorite Miles Davis album, on the stereo, wanting Max to hear beautiful music. While it was still warm out, Mark carried Max outside, wanting him to feel a soft summer breeze on his cheeks. Mark held Max, resting the infant's bare chest against his, as Max seemed to calm at the feel of skin against skin.

As the evening darkened, Max's breathing grew more labored. I changed him into our favorite outfit, sat with him in my arms on the couch, and sang "Silent Night" to him. It grew close to 11:00 pm, and I could feel his time with us was nearing an end. I felt scared to see him die and even more scared to feel him die. I didn't want to be the one holding him when he died. I didn't want to feel his body stop moving, feel his warmth cool, hear the silence when he stopped breathing, see his stillness. I handed Max to Mark to hold next to me and continued to touch him and hum to him.

A few minutes later, Max lifted his arms to us in what we would later learn was a physical reflex, but felt to us like a desire for one last hug. He drew his last breath and died. Mark and I both cried for an hour or more. We wrapped Max in his fleecy pastel baby blanket and laid him for the first time in his crib in his bedroom. It was the only night he would spend in his room.

I went to bed and cried instead of slept all night, imagining terrible scenes, like flies landing on my baby's corpse in the next room. When the funeral home came to pick up my baby the next day, I snipped a lock of his hair to keep for myself before letting them take him.

When I finally returned to work after my maternity leave with only pictures to show my coworkers, I placed a framed photo of Max on my desk. It was a close-up of his serene face soon after he'd been born, his eyes eternally closed, a baby cap covering the open wound on his head. You could see the fuzz of downy hair on his rounded cheek.

I found that I drew strength when I looked at his picture. I aspired each day to be more like Max—to be bolder in my embrace of life, to be more fearless, to be more accepting of the harsh realities of life. If my four-and-a-half-day-old infant could meet his demise and go so fearlessly into the night, surely I could do the same someday.

I wasn't as brave yet as I aspired to be. I hadn't been brave enough to hold my baby while he died and I felt ashamed of that. But I was braver than I thought. I'd been brave enough to love him. I'd been brave enough to let him go.

MY GREEK FATHER, A BACON CHEESEBURGER DELUXE, AND A BOY FROM QUEENS

By Elizabeth M. Economou

IN THE SUMMER OF 2001, A FORMER PUNTER FOR THE NFL blew in like a nor'easter and asked me to marry him six months after our first date on Super Bowl Sunday in New York City. By contrast, my father, a Greek immigrant, had courted my mother, a petite, classic beauty nine years his junior for nearly a decade before he proposed.

Wearing khakis and flip-flops, my California-based fiancé reached inside his pocket for an engagement ring with 17 itty-bitty baguettes, the same number he wore as a walk-on in the 1980s. He hastily popped the question followed by: "I've got to move on with my life." Not exactly the way I'd pictured this moment, but in my late thirties, I was willing to overlook things I might not have in the past.

Four years earlier at thirty-three, a middle-school English teacher, I'd moved out of my parents' home in Seattle—for the *first time ever*—to take a fluke TV writing job at a cable news channel in Midtown Manhattan, a high-octane commercial district where some 700,000 commuters shuttle in and out every day. Leaving my close-knit family for Gotham—which might as well have been Mars as far as my parents were concerned—was heart-wrenching, but the price I was willing to pay for my late blooming independence. Instantly, I'd fallen madly in love with my newly adopted city, but my old world paradigm and traditional values clashed with the racy dating scene, something I didn't want any part of despite being single and available.

"Okay, yeah, sure, I guess so," I said to the punter, equivocally. Aside from living thousands of miles away, he was a nice enough guy. I'd met him in my early teens at a youth basketball tournament. Both from the West Coast and of Greek heritage—though my parents were born in the old country while his were from the states—we'd run into each over the years at various Hellenic-related events. In early 2000, we unexpectedly crossed paths again, this time in my Upper East Side neighborhood where I was living and working.

Disappointed he hadn't asked my father for his blessing, "I need to call mom and dad right away," I said, walking out of the living room, shaking my head. The punter should've known better, I thought. He owed them that.

"Are you sure about this?" asked my mother, "Is he worthy of you?" They wanted me married, but to the right person.

"Be careful," warned my father, a man of few words, albeit wise.

Deep in my gut, I knew that our relationship wasn't going to be the kind of love that simmers slowly and builds to an I-can't-live-without-you crescendo as my parents' love had done. Still, I had a shot at "happily ever after." What's more, my spinster days were coming to an end. Who was I to want more?

Instead of savoring the moment, my cross-country fiancé wanted to set the date, right then and there. Moving at viral speed, he was a bullet train bound for the altar.

❖

In 1959, my parents, both immigrants, wed in a traditional Greek Orthodox ceremony. My father donned a black tuxedo with satin piping while my mother beamed in an ivory gown with a scalloped-neckline. Every year on their anniversary in October, he'd send her long-stemmed roses with clusters of baby's breath that looked like snow. They came in a shiny gold box with a satiny red ribbon—just like in the movies.

Dad never missed a romantic beat.

At Christmas time even when he couldn't break away from the restaurant, he'd send me or my sisters to the shopping mall to buy mom an elegantly wrapped Chanel No. 5 gift set, the kind with fancy perfume and silky white powder. He wanted her to have something special from him under the tree.

On Mother's Day, he'd select two orchid corsages from the high-class florist near his blue-collar restaurant. He gave one to my mom and the other to my grandmother, his mother-in-law, to wear them to church that day.

My parents were married for forty-two years until my father's sudden passing, shortly after 9/11 just a few months after the punter and I got engaged. Not surprisingly, when dad departed this life, a part of my mother left with him.

As a teenager during WWII, amid the Nazi occupation of Aegina, an island near Athens where he was born and raised, my father smuggled lemons and olive oil, risking his life to help feed his family.

Similarly, in all my years of living at home, I never saw my dad walk through the front door without a bag of groceries. "When you shop, shop heavy," he'd say. The consummate provider, he filled our lives much the same way he filled our pantry: with sweetness and abundance. And now—with the seventeen-stoned ring on my hand—I realized that all along I'd been waiting for someone like him.

Though my father, a restaurant owner and cook, was calm and steady despite a life of toil, the punter was argumentative and emotional. Out for dinner one night, he berated me publicly about everything and nothing. And I wondered how we'd build a life together when we couldn't even agree on which salad to order at the Italian restaurant with the blue awning. The object of his derision, I—still reeling from my dad's passing—couldn't bear to lose him, but for all the wrong reasons. Dad's loss was shocking and dark. The mere thought of losing someone close to me seemed unbearable—even if that someone was zapping whatever light I had left inside me.

Still, he pressured me to marry him right away. Ever since losing his father, he longed for a family of his own. But with my dad's recent passing, I couldn't see a wedding in my immediate future, not before properly mourning him, not before his one year memorial. It was time to grieve, not celebrate.

Eventually, the emotional gulf between us eclipsed thousands of miles that separated us physically. "We're done," he said over the telephone from 2,800 miles away "I've got to move on with my life" His words rang eerily familiar.

Haste had coursed through our engagement from the outset, and it was ending in much the same way. The punter, it seemed, was more in love with the idea of marriage than with me—by Thanksgiving, he'd wed another. And I should have known better than to gamble with my heart—despite my age. Still, I was equally to blame for the way things turned out.

In the months that followed, I focused on my widowed mother—flying back to Seattle when I could—and on my job as a publicist to a classical music producer. When the hurt in my heart seemed to vanish like rain drops on scorching pavement, I scuttled up nine flights of stairs to the post office at Macy's flagship in Herald Square. As I dropped my engagement ring into the clunky mailbox, relief washed over me like a sudden burst of shade on a long humid run. And I felt lighter as if could soar way above the Empire State Building.

❖

On the day I turned thirty-nine, my twin sister Eva phoned to wish me "Happy Birthday" from a lively piazza in Rome. While she and her beloved sipped Limoncello, I sat alone, eating cereal in my tiny loft-like studio. From my window, I watched giddy couples go by though I was anything but. I recalled a line from a Woody Allen movie: "Your life is the sum of all your choices" and I questioned my purpose, and once again, my singleness. And like Socrates had urged, I was examining my life from every possible angle, but coming up dry.

Days later, I bumped into George, a brawny pharmacist from Astoria, Queens, on the corner of 69th Street and First Avenue on my way home from work. We talked for longer than I expected—the cacophonous sound of rush-hour traffic blaring all around us.

The son of Greek immigrants, he worked for a retail drugstore chain in my neighborhood. Passionate about his mortar-and-pestle profession, he delivered meds to ailing customers on his own time.

I'd met him several months earlier in my neighborhood at the Holy Trinity Greek Orthodox where we both attended. From the outset, there was something inherently familiar about him—as if there was never a time when we didn't know each other. We talked at length at coffee hours and over lunch a few times, up until my month-long work trip to Athens, Greece.

Though nothing romantic had started between us, I remember telling my twin sister how kind-hearted he was. But that's all. I was leaving for a while, and I didn't want to start something only to be riddled with heartache—or rejection—overseas.

Like the punter, George had also lost his father at a young age. But unlike the punter and very much like my dad, he was a black belt in delaying gratification. On his own from his late teens he'd gone more than a decade-and-a-half without a vacation. And I filed that away like someone would a golden treasure.

In early September—fatigued and jet lagged—I stumbled into the drugstore, where George worked, hoping he'd be there.

"Welcome back," he said. "Love the tan."

Later that evening, Eddie, the all-knowing doorman, buzzed.

"Some guy named George is here to see you," he said.

I opened the door and there he stood clutching a bouquet of roses and stargazer lilies in one hand, and a bacon cheeseburger deluxe from the diner near my apartment in the other. "Thought you could use the protein," he said, still in his white lab coat.

From that moment on, we were a couple.

For my fortieth birthday, nine months later, George surprised me with a party. A few weeks after that, while I was Windexing the bathroom mirror, he proposed; but this time, I had no reservations, no anxiety. And I felt blessed beyond measure as if my prayers had been answered—as if George was too good to be true.

Shortly after we were engaged, my mother was diagnosed with stomach cancer. George was by my side every step of the way. For three nights, he slept on the dank floor in the hospital waiting area wrapped in a tattered sheet with a soiled sofa cushion under his head. "There's no place I'd rather be," he said. A week later, the surgeon gave us his prognosis: "the cancer had not spread." George squeezed my hand as tears trickled down my face.

They say that women tend to marry men like their fathers, and I couldn't help but note the similarities between George and my dad. Beyond earning a living by standing, never wearing jeans, and drinking amber-colored Greek brandy, they both assumed responsibility with dignity and sacrificed to make others happy.

Just shy of my 41st birthday, George and I walked down the aisle as husband and wife, both of us for the very first time. And if my dad had been alive, I'm certain he would have given us his blessing, especially for waiting to find the right person— as he had done.

FINISHED

By Kellini Walter

I SCANNED MY BLUE BADGE AND HEARD *QUA-THUNK, CLICK*. The sound of the sequence was so familiar to me that I didn't even really hear it anymore. For thirteen years and four months, I swiped my blue badge against the three-by-four-inch black card readers across the Microsoft campus and waited for the red light to blink green and signal my permission to enter. And now I had finally scanned it for the last time.

As I walked to human resources to turn in my laptop, my badge, and my corporate American Express card, I was gripped by the power this place had over my life. I stopped and leaned against the wall to remember.

I had been glad to be at Microsoft in October 1998, when I first walked through the doors of Building 20 for my new-employee orientation. At that point there were approximately 32,000 employees, and people who had worked at Microsoft had gotten rich off stock options. I wasn't sure if that would happen to me, but I was coming back from five years of working from home. I was glad to have somewhere to go in the morning and something to do all day long. And after falling backward from a master's degree in psychology to a career in business, I was really happy to be at a place where people were so smart and I could learn more than any MBA program could teach me.

About a week after I started, I drove over to another part of campus for my first big meeting. I walked into the two-story cafeteria nestled among the five massive buildings of the RedWest (Redmond West) campus. RedWest was the only satellite campus at that point—the main campus housed about 20 buildings.

· *We Came Back to Say* ·

I nearly got vertigo as I looked down the long expanse of the natural stone staircase. A cacophonous echo made me feel like I was at a dizzy marketplace in a Third World country. Before I started down the steps, I looked up at the massive, solid wood beams that framed the ceiling, perfectly expressing contemporary Pacific Northwest architecture.

At the bottom of the stairs was a discreet set of double doors that opened into a small entryway about ten feet wide and as deep. A second set of doors then opened into a quiet tomb of a conference room buried deep in the stone walls of this extravagant building.

I took my seat and looked around the table. Out of the twenty or so people in the room, about three quarters were men from their mid to late thirties. I was thirty-five at the time and had never found guys in the corporate world that attractive. In this context I still didn't. They were normal to nice-looking guys in khakis and button-down shirts. I sat down and imagined closets with rows and rows of perfectly pressed khaki pants, much better brands than Dockers, and lightly starched shirts. The bravest amongst them had different colored or patterned shirts, or maybe some wacky socks.

The few women in the room didn't bunch up around one consistent fashion choice. The one that appeared to be the most senior person in the room (based on how people buzzed around her) had her auburn hair piled in an intricate up-do like something a bride would wear.

The toughest woman in the room spoke with a gravelly voice but had thick fingers that were tipped with perfect, French manicured acrylic nails. And there was boisterous kid-sister type who, it seemed to me, would go out and kick around a soccer ball with the boys when we were done. Soccer lady was wearing jeans and a T-shirt and everyone called her by her Microsoft alias, which was the first letter of her first name (S for Sarah) followed by the first seven letters of her last name (NICKERSon). It came out as SNICKERS, like she was a candy bar.

As we all took seats around the table, one of the khakis handed out a thick packet of paper. It was very detailed set of data that covered most of the page, sandwiched between text boxes in the margins that attempted to bring some order to what otherwise looked like chaos.

By the time everyone settled around the table with their packets it was 1:15 p.m. The meeting was scheduled to last until 5:00 p.m. We began to review page one—out of thirty-nine.

The goal of the meeting was to manage the inventory levels, i.e. how much product would be built for the holiday sales season. There wasn't any clear principle or philosophy, like it's better to over-build and not stock out, or it's OK to stock out and lose sales if we don't have to destroy excess inventory. In the absence of these types of guard rails, we spent an hour on that first page and roamed around an infinite number of "what if" scenarios. No clear decisions were made.

At 4:25 p.m., we were on page twelve of the packet and had begun to review the products that I was responsible for. I didn't realize what was about to happen, or that I was minutes away from surrendering my most profound super-power. It was super important for me to fit in and offer something meaningful to this process, so I found my voice and shared my opinion: that it would be better to risk over-building than stocking out because the cost of inventory was lower than the gross margin of the products (which is rarely the case with consumer products). One of the nicer and smarter Khakis, who would later become my favorite president of my favorite division at the company, listened to me. I went on to say how much inventory I thought we should build and another Khaki asked me the basis of that forecast. I gave the most honest answer possible, "it's a gut sense."

"You need a better reason than that," was all Ms. Up-do had to say about it. But it was enough. If I was going to succeed, and I did very much want to succeed, I would have to learn how to make something called data-driven decisions. Even though I didn't know what that meant.

I had always made most of my decisions based on how I felt, but this style of thinking my way around a question wasn't completely unnatural to me. I occupy vast spaces in my head more often than any other spaces. So I learned. And the seemingly genuine urgency of all those meetings, all those debates, all those spreadsheets, and all those PowerPoint presentations was so tantalizing, so seductive.

Quickly I learned to believe that I was now somehow in a race, and that I needed to run faster and smarter than anyone else because, well, at Microsoft we seemed to run the fastest in the race of self-achievement. I honed my analytical skills. I perfected my abilities to anticipate what questions I'd be asked. I went in early and stayed late. I become a mother and still I kept going. I kept advancing. It was intoxicating.

Until I failed.

Mid-way through my time as an FTE (full time employee) in the fall of 2005, I was in charge of the marketing strategy for $1 billion (B) of a $13B portfolio of products. That may sound like a big deal, but no one is ever really in charge of anything—in life or at Microsoft. And, it was an unnecessarily tangled problem because anything I recommended would impact other aspects of the business. So my job was to build a strategy that would optimize the $1B without doing any harm to the other $12B.

Over six months, I chewed through the business challenges. I sat through hundreds of hours of meetings and listened to a bunch of super smart people tell me what the right answer was—from their perspective. Yet everyone's individual perspective, while always answering a part of the puzzle, couldn't solve the big picture. I did it. And then I had to sell it in to the president of the division.

Things started to slide south a couple of hours before the meeting. Despite the months I had spent building the strategy, the weeks I had spent socializing the plan, and the days I had spent agonizing over the perfect way to present it, I found myself completely tongue-tied and terrified. I didn't know what I wanted to say or how I was going to start the meeting. I stood up to rehearse.

"As you know James (the king Khaki/ president), we have some difficult challenges. We need to drive growth in the consumer packaged product without cannibalizing the enterprise revenue. We also need to … " At this point I got distracted and my mind felt like an explosion of thoughts all flying around like ping pong balls in one of those lottery machines on TV. I had inexplicably lost the ability to reach in, pull out, and string together a set of thoughts. So I paced. And practiced. And floated out of my body.

As I stood outside of the conference room waiting I began to feel better. It was time to just get this over with. Then my boss's boss leaned over to me. "Remind me again why we think it's OK to lose money?"

From the scrunched-up look of his eyes, I knew this was not a good question. It was not a, "Hey, I'm confident in your plan, just run me through it one more time." It was a, "I have only paid attention to a small number of the gestures you have made to prepare me for this meeting, and now I'm not really sure this is a good idea."

In my head I responded, "Because last fucking week when you reviewed this plan, you agreed that we had to release the product into the OEM channel and that would create cannibalization in the near term but protect us from long-term competitive threats. You were there, you weighed in. And now, right now when we are walking into the room, you are questioning the riskiest aspect of the recommendation?"

But out loud I froze. "Uh, because there's too much long-term risk if we don't," I managed. He was an unusually kind executive, but I always wondered if he was going to unzip his face and let an alien lizard spring forth.

James came in late and sat at the top of the horseshoe seating arrangement in the room. I slowly started to croak out my rehearsed opening. I was awkward enough that a couple of the nine other people in the room looked down at the floor. James started to flip ahead through the presentation.

After a few minutes, I caught my breath and started to get in the flow of my words. Then Jeff stopped me. "Kellini, are you telling me that we need to lose $70,000?"

"Well, I'm telling you that there's a lot of long-term risk if we don't take a hit in the short term."

"OK. But do you think I got up this morning thinking to myself, 'I want to go into work today so Kellini can tell me we need to lose money of this business?'"

I was stunned. $70,000 in a $13B business is something that would commonly be referred to as a rounding error.

I started to shake, and the fan that blew the ping pong balls of thoughts around in my head came on full blast. I was searching, reaching, for anything to bring this conversation back to a reasonable place. I searched the eyes across the room and pleaded for someone to say something so I could take a break and pull myself back together. The lizard head just blinked (were those two eyelids?) quietly. The four peers that had helped me build the plan looked down at their feet. Metaphorical business crickets chirped to highlight the long silence. I took a deep breath.

"It's just that we believe," (and by *we* I mean the people that are sitting on their hands looking at their feet and saying nothing right now) "that there is a long-term competitive threat if the OEMs start to pre-install competitive productivity tools."

James' voice was ridiculously thick with condescension. "But Kellini, you didn't build a model that shows the current baseline changing over time. You built a model that shows a steady baseline. Only an idiot would argue that this model shows long-term risk."

I had finally pulled myself together. Being called an idiot pissed me off.

"Sure. OK. Fine. There are a lot of variables in play and rather than debate several assumptions, I wanted to show the worst-case scenario—what this strategy would mean against the current baseline."

He looked down at his watch. "Are we about finished? I have to catch a helicopter to the airport. Do it the right way and come back in a few weeks."

Then, even as his business manager started to remind him that he still had thirty minutes before the helicopter was picking him up on the roof, he stood up and walked out.

Lizard face started to talk. "Well that didn't quite go the way we had hoped, but we will live to fight another day … " I tried to listen but I had to will myself to stay pulled together until I could fall apart.

When we wrapped up, I moved as quickly as possible out the door and down the hall to the safety of my office. On my way one of the senior Khakis from the meeting walked up next to me and leaned in quietly. "In the future I need you to make sure I'm better prepared before we go in front of James. I felt really exposed in there."

Up until that moment, I had been able to keep my shame suspended. But now anger welled up like a fiery knot in my throat.

"Are you fucking serious?" I ran through an entire angry diatribe inside my head. *"I invited you to multiple meetings that you blew off. And you sat there and said absolutely nothing. James probably didn't even know you were there because the only person he was focused on undoing in that meeting was me. And I just completely leveled the landscape of my career. And you feel exposed? Are you really that self-absorbed?"*

But I could feel the dam of tears starting to burst so I just stared straight ahead and said, "Sure. Fine. Whatever you need."

There are very few moments in life where I have felt squeezed so tight that it seems like I literally become dislodged from where I thought I was and I emerge in some new and foreign place. The next few hours were a blur of emotional arcs that diverged in many directions despite being rooted in the same place: fear.

I couldn't bear to go back. I had to start looking for another job immediately. How would I support my family?

Finally, the quiet voice of my intuition spoke up. *"This isn't finished with you yet. You have to go back."* I realized this quiet voice had been guiding me all along. I would have to redeem myself or I might never recover—on the inside. I would take this and keep going.

Late that night I laid curled up in bed next to the partner I adored, and I looked at the note my daughters had left for me—we love you mommy, it will all be ok. And it would. But in that moment I knew that everything has changed. I couldn't go back in the old way and not suffer. So I tried to sleep—and waited for a new day.

Everything did change. I eventually took a different job, one where I could write more and be more creative, more intuitive. It slowed my career growth down, but I didn't care. I worked and plodded and waited for the moment when I knew it was finally time to go.

And finally, six-and-half years later, on February 1, 2012, I stopped reminiscing, leaned away from the wall and willed myself to keep walking to human resources. And I smiled at the thought that Microsoft had brought me so many good things.

But I had seen it through, and it was finally finished with me.

ME, MY WEIGHT, AND I

By Dana Montanari

LIKE LUNG CANCER CATCHING UP WITH A SMOKER, morbid obesity caught up with me. Initially, it found me as a college girl trying to fit into too-small jeans and offered me luscious ice cream bars, fresh salsas with crisp, salty tortilla chips, and bacon cheeseburgers. It returned when my fiancé broke off our engagement and offered me grilled T-bone steaks and seasoned thick-cut fries. Later, it snuck in disguised as a compassionate friend when I moved 3,000 miles from Seattle to Boston and was introduced to a tempting menu of Italian subs, black and white frappes, and deep-fried Chinese food delicacies.

I never wanted to be fat, obese, overweight, big-boned, thick, stocky, stout, or boxy. When I was deep in the dating scene, I wanted to sit on my boyfriend's lap without worrying about crushing his legs. When I was backpacking through Europe and arrived at the French Riviera, I wanted to wear a bikini, not a one-piece swimsuit. When I was beginning my career, I wanted to wear a classic shift dress and have extra room swimming around my hips. When I was a bride-to-be, I wanted to be slender enough to be carried over the threshold. None of my wishes came true.

In my early twenties, on a crisp October day, I sat in the University of Washington's Red Square patiently waiting for my prospective boyfriend Mitch to show up. I had worked hard to look fashionable in my eighties-wear—black slouchy boots, black tights, a salt-and-pepper-speckled miniskirt, and a purple cashmere sweater. I hoped that these adornments, coupled with my kinky-permed blonde mane of hair and a recent, heavy spritz of the latest popular perfume, would convince Mitch that I was beautiful once he joined me at our second meeting. Based on how we'd met, I simply hoped he'd recognize me.

Our first encounter consisted of me, in a drunken stupor, crashing his fraternity party with a gaggle of girlfriends as we tried to hide our "commuter student" status—we didn't exactly belong in UW's Greek Row. I danced maniacally around Delta Something Something House's makeshift dance floor and drank unfortunate amounts of the punch cum ninety percent Everclear 151, which gave me the bravery needed to offer Mitch a flirty kiss before slipping him my phone number. Certainly, the heady combination of lust, liquor, and the lack of condoms available that night propelled Mitch back to me that second time.

The second date was heavenly. We walked around the beautiful campus breathing in the autumn air and each other. He held my hand, we laughed at each other's jokes, and we made plans for the upcoming weekend. He later told me that when he saw me waiting for him that day, he sat down and watched me from afar for a few minutes before approaching, marveling at his good fortune in meeting me.

Mitch came from a good family. His father was a university professor in Ohio and his mother, a stay-at-home mom, was a chocolate chip cookie-making aficionado whose cookies would make cookie company executives wish they knew her secret ingredient. He spoke of his younger sister with great affection and admiration. He was studying to be a doctor. He was quite a catch.

Those first months, Mitch and I spent hours on the phone during the week and were together every weekend night. As we gazed into each other's adoring eyes one night, he said, "Dana, you are almost perfect. You know what would make you perfect?" I thought of many things but what he said hadn't entered my mind.

He looked deeply into my eyes and whispered, "If you lost just five pounds, you'd be perfect."

I believed him.

At 5'8" tall, I weighed 150 pounds and played college tennis. I was ranked fourth in the state for my community college division. My athletic success did little to bolster my confidence; it did not provide me with the mettle to tell him off or break up with him. Instead, in my typical people-pleaser persona, I thought, *Doesn't everyone strive for perfection? This guy really likes me; he's just looking out for my best interest.*

So began my roller coaster-diet life. I starved myself all day and, once the sun went down, I rewarded myself with a huge bowl of ice cream—mentally noting that if those were the only calories I consumed, I would lose weight. My body graciously rewarded me with a five-pound weight gain.

Eventually, Mitch and I broke up. But by then, the kernels of my dysfunctional relationship with food were firmly planted.

Not long after the breakup, I met Roger. At first glance, Roger did not appear to be dating material. We met in French class and his accent was atrocious. It was so bad that the professor suggested that Roger consider taking a Germanic language to take advantage of his "guttural utterances." He was a strapping 6'2", wavy-haired, blue-eyed California boy with an affinity for T-bone steaks and rich, high-fat ice cream. The worn, brown label on his jeans proclaimed he sported a 32-inch waist and a 38-inch inseam. Read: slim waist, long legs.

Roger badgered me for months to date him. Eventually, I gave in.

He arrived for our first date in his black pick-up truck wearing a freshly pressed flannel shirt, spit-shined snakeskin cowboy boots, and those well-fitting jeans. I was breathless when I saw the bouquet of purple irises in his hand. His usually unruly hair was controlled with gel and the smell of his masculine cologne hung heavy in the air. On the way to dinner, he told me about his last relationship.

"She nearly broke me when she ran off to Europe with the dance troupe. I didn't think I could care about someone again. But you, you're different. Sweet...and kind. I think I could love you." Even though I was uncertain about how I felt about him, his words made me feel cared for, longed for, desired. He took a small piece of my heart home with him that night and, not long afterwards, I gave him the rest.

After we'd been dating for a year, the honeymoon period began to fade. After many consecutive dinners of meat and potatoes followed by personal pints of ice cream, I could no longer maintain my tennis weight.

Though we didn't live together, I spent almost every night at Roger's. One summer evening, we snuggled in for a long night of me watching him play video games on his TV in the dark. We talked about our future and what our marriage "requirements" were. I murmured something about loving one another forever and my hope to have several children. His requirements were more specific.

"I've been meaning to talk to you about a few things. If we are going to make it in the long term, there are a few things I'd change."

"Like what?" I was more than curious.

"Um, your nose, for instance. You know I love you, but your nose, well…when we're rich, I'll pay for you to get a nose job."

My nose? Typically my worries were limited to the flatness of my stomach—or lack thereof—and the circumference of my thighs. I had never considered that my nose might be problematic.

"Anything else?"

"Yes. I really don't like it when you wear red. It looks bad on you."

My favorite color looks bad on me? This was getting very personal.

"Is that all?"

"It looks like you've put on a few pounds since we got together. It's really hard to be attracted to you when you're chubby. If this is going to be long term, you're gonna hafta do something about those double-digit jeans of yours. I can't see myself married to a fat woman. You understand, right, Hon?" He gave me a sweet smile, chuckled, and sealed it with a kiss. Like that made it better.

"Am I to understand that fifteen pounds over my ideal weight makes me fat?" I refrained from screaming, though the words were echoing in my head.

"I know you can lose the weight. I'd love to see you in those size 8 jeans! That would be perfect. Then I could cup your butt right in my hand. Mmmhmm." I knew I'd heard that perfection line before—some other time, some other boy. Though my body wanted to rebel, in my mind, I believed him.

Three and a half years later, Roger broke off our engagement—three months before the wedding. I moved out of our shared home back to my mother's house with only my 30-pound weight gain to comfort me. If being overweight repelled Roger, then surely being skinny would attract him and others. I stopped eating for a time. After I'd lost 40 pounds and weighed 142, my best friend Marika seemed concerned.

"You look anorexic."

"I'm not anorexic. That's ridiculous. I'm wearing size 8 jeans, that's in the normal range for my height and weight." I felt a surge of pride inside when I mentioned the single-digit sizing.

"Well, you don't look like yourself."

I didn't really know what I was supposed to look like. It didn't matter what I did, someone always commented about why my weight wasn't right.

Six months after my broken engagement, I met Mike at a party put on by some friends from high school; we hit it off immediately. Originally from Wellesley, Massachusetts, an affluent suburb of Boston, he was living and working in Seattle and playing hockey a couple nights per week. He had Irish looks and an Italian attitude, loved baseball primarily but followed every sport, and thought his parents were fun. One year older than me, we shared a love of alternative nineties music, spending time on the coast, and taking back roads home instead of the busy highway. He was handy with electrical problems and carpentry, liked Mexican food, and cats (swoon). Mike's directness, raw masculinity, and infectious laugh were unlike the typical West Coast boys I'd dated. He accepted me at 142 pounds and also at 180 pounds. He said he loved me when I hit 201 pounds and never expressed any disdain when I hit my peak after gaining more than 60 additional pounds.

One night during lovemaking, his fingertips grazed my abdomen, startling me.

"What's wrong?" he asked.

"Uh, I am very uncomfortable with my body. I feel fat."

"You're not, you're perfect." He kissed me and held me close.

Over the course of the next year, Mike and I packed up our Seattle lives, moved to Boston, and eloped. When something's right, it's right. Nineteen years later, we are still together and I still struggle with my weight.

Five years ago, when I was in my late thirties, I stepped on the scale. It was one year after I'd given birth to my second son. The scale glared

267 pounds. It wasn't the 267 number that bothered me; it was the 33 pounds shy of 300 that made me gasp.

When I saw my all-time high of 267 on the scale, I imagined an "About Me" on my blog that described me as follows: green-eyed Human Resources executive, memory like a steel trap, morbidly obese, likes cats. I thought about depressing trips to "big girl" stores devoid of fashionable clothing as I remembered my devastation during my extensive search for cute and appropriate plus-size, career-girl maternity wear.

I ignored my doctor's not-so-subtle hints that I was on a collision course with chronic problems.

"Dana, are you aware that if you continue to gain weight you are at risk for polycystic ovaries, joint pain and eventual joint replacements, pre-diabetes, gall bladder disease, and thyroid trouble?"

"Um, no."

My doctor was right (there, I said it). I eventually had my gall bladder removed following months of considerable abdominal pain and, three months after that, had a pre-cancerous tumor removed—along with the right side of my thyroid, in which the tumor had been nesting.

I had gained 117 pounds in the twenty years since my high school graduation. Once I got to that place, I felt coated in a veneer of shame that covered every thought, every physical movement, every social interaction I had. Obesity crept up on me one day at a time, one French fry at a time.

The signs were there all along. I ignored them. One day, I looked in the mirror and there, looking back at me, was my shapeless chin and my chin's chin. I noticed a budding roll of fat just above the waistline of my jeans that seemingly appeared overnight and my bra cut a deep line into my back, causing me to be short of breath. I stood there wondering how in the world I got to this place—this place of embarrassment, this place of anxiety, this place of no going back to my high school weight and my size 8 jeans. I knew the clothes I'd kept for fifteen years would never fit again, though I continued to save them, always thinking that *maybe next year* would be the one when I would have my shit together and the miniskirt would look good again. At my age, and in my executive job, a miniskirt was surely out of the question anyway, but no matter. I thought for the millionth time that

I would start a diet tomorrow and made a mental list of the things I would not eat—no sugar, no soda, no pizza, no Mexican food. I thought I needed to learn to love whole grains, dandelion greens, detox tea, and running half marathons.

As an obese person, I'd come to look at life through a filter that I thought was unique to being fat. I lived through disapproving shop clerks in boutique stores asking if I was there to buy a scarf, because they didn't have a plus-size department. On a six-hour flight to California, a flight attendant mentioned that, "once the seatbelt extender reaches its maximum, customers need to consider purchasing two seats." And there were other things: the cysts that developed in the crevices and folds of my girth; the doctor who told me I'd have more money if I spent it on a gym membership and not junk food; and a well-meaning friend who said I would look great in a new shirt if I would, "like, lose maybe five pounds."

What was my response to the criticism and the pain? I masked it. Many nights on my way home from work, I stopped at my favorite restaurant and ate the boneless buffalo wings and thick steak fries I loved. With the first bite, I would feel a sense of calm overcome me. It was a lovely feeling. Though ashamed of my behavior (I felt like a closet alcoholic), I would eat every last bite and wash it down with a big strawberry lemonade. Once I arrived home, I would tell my husband that I'd had a late lunch and wouldn't need dinner.

I wonder why people who have just a few pounds to lose complain so bitterly about it or make light-hearted comments about cellulite. I have a hard time talking about such a personally painful subject so I don't generally volunteer my thoughts about my weight loss issues. If I laugh gently along with them, maybe they will think I am one of them—a skinny girl deep down inside.

But if asked, I would tell them that my extra body armor makes it hard to walk up steep downtown Seattle hills and that my joints ache after an "easy" thirty-minute walk, which then results in a two-hour nap the minute I get home. I would tell them that when you're obese, exercise does not, in fact, make you feel energetic; it makes you feel like dying. I would share how awful it was to acknowledge that I hadn't lost the baby weight from my first pregnancy and about the sad day I donated my extensive shoe collection to charity because my feet were too fat for them. I would explain that I can't go for a bike ride around town or take an aerobics class with a friend on Saturday because I don't have the stamina for either one. Because I am fat. And I would tell them that I wish every day that I only had a few pounds to lose, not 100.

"Dana, you should come to my running group tonight," says one of my mommy-group friends, a self-proclaimed "Triathlon Freak."

"You know, Sasha, it's just not something I am capable of. I am trying to do the treadmill right now and am not ready for running."

"Come on, you can do it!"

"No, really, I don't think I could get through it."

"Dana, you can do it!"

"Well, my knees are a little weak right now but I am working on strengthening them. Maybe in a couple months."

"Ah, I know you can do it…"

No really, I'm thinking, *I can't fucking do it.*

But maybe someday soon.

FISHING IN DEATH VALLEY
By Jennifer Crowder

I stood poised with a stopwatch, intently focused on a tiny fish—a Death Valley pupfish—swimming in a small, deep pool almost completely hidden by a tumble of rocks. Another fish swerved to meet it, and they hovered together, briefly motionless, before darting off in opposite directions. The instant I saw them come together, I'd clicked the stopwatch on, and then clicked it again when they separated. Reading the result, I started to record it on my worksheet, where it would join a long column of numbers. But the pencil snagged on the paper, dampened by my sweaty hands, and tore a hole in it. "Shit!" I muttered.

I paused and looked around; the few other volunteers within sight were all absorbed in their tasks. I craved company, someone to talk with. What was I doing here, anyway? Spending a day in the desert gathering data for a study on endangered fish was not among the activities I'd envisioned for my freshman year of college. But then again, I'd had no idea what to expect. I'd taken a big risk coming here—I'd visited just once, late the preceding spring. I was over 1,000 miles from home. And I knew no one. But that meant no one knew me, either. And that was the point: I could reinvent myself.

Footsteps crunched on the rocks behind me. "How's it going?" asked Conor, one of the study's graduate assistants. I'd made the four-hour trip here from Claremont with my friend Wendy, who'd persuaded me to join her that day, in the cab of an old Ford pickup driven by Conor. On the way, he'd described growing up in Southern California, a Newport Beach surf bum. His laconic style gave the impression of being stoned. Maybe he was, but he also seemed to be extraordinarily intelligent.

"Hey, Conor. It's going great—except I've just trashed this worksheet."

"Don't worry about it—it doesn't have to be gorgeous, just readable," Conor replied, tilting my clipboard so he could see my notations. "Hey, you've got a busy pool. Lots of good data. Horny little devils, aren't they?"

His laugh faded quickly in the dry, hot air as he moved on to check with the next volunteer. *This day has been surreal,* I thought to myself, lifting my gaze to the distant mountains, shimmering and undulating in the desert heat. I resumed my task. Here I was, just two months into my freshman year at Scripps College, east of Los Angeles in Claremont—an English major with mountains of reading to do. Instead, I was observing pupfish mating behavior in Death Valley.

Granted, the fish *are* remarkable—in the solar-heated pools they inhabit, the water can reach 112 degrees and may be two to three times saltier than sea water. Their world is limited to a narrow, horizontal band of water that maintains a specific temperature range. Outside this rarefied ecosystem, the fish can't survive. It can be too hot near the surface, too cool deeper down. *They're choosy about their neighborhood,* I thought. I could appreciate that.

The spare, unforgiving desert landscape emphasized how far I was from my home in the temperate marine climate of Washington's Puget Sound region. I'd left Seattle just a few months earlier to start college. Much as I loved the Northwest, I was fascinated by what local radio announcers called "The Southland," the LA basin, with its appalling smog, endless traffic, rampant crime—and some of the friendliest, most open people I'd ever met.

On that day in Death Valley, I was even more taken with the desert, with its long, open sightlines and expansive sky. I remember sensing an essential shift in my center of balance. The new environment was changing my perspective. *This is good,* I told myself.

Six months earlier, when I knew Scripps only as a name on an application, I'd had no idea where I'd end up. Like most of my peers graduating from our suburban high school in the late 70s, I didn't know what I wanted to do with my life—I knew only that I'd attend college somewhere. That was a family expectation I'd never questioned.

I'd applied to schools across the country and had been accepted by most. A favorite English teacher had recommended Scripps, a small women's college that is part of a larger consortium known as the Claremont Colleges.

When my Great Uncle Paul learned I was considering Scripps, he'd written to recommend the school. "They graduate smart, strong, independent women," he'd commented. My family all respected Uncle Paul, my grandfather's older brother, who lived in Palo Alto and had been a scriptwriter for a popular western TV series. He'd become familiar with Scripps while spending a summer at the Claremont Graduate School years earlier.

Still, never having lived anywhere but in the Seattle area, I was intimidated by the prospect of such a major change. Southern California seemed very distant, the college an abstraction. My only memory of LA came from an epic cross-country family vacation one summer in the early 70s. We'd visited Disneyland, camping in a borrowed tent trailer near the park. The campground was located on a former orange grove, and my sister and I had picked oranges from one of the few trees left.

I'd also been accepted at University of Washington, just a half hour from my parents' home on the east side of Lake Washington. It was much easier to envision myself there. Most of my friends were going to the UW; it seemed to be the default choice. I wasn't in love with the idea of a big university, but in the absence of any other familiar choice, the thought of remaining close to my home, parents, family, and friends was comforting.

Well, *mostly* comforting. I felt uneasy knowing that my high school boyfriend would be in the area, too, finishing his senior year. Our breakup just months before my graduation had left me despondent in the way only the ending of a first relationship can.

He wasn't a bad person, exactly—we were both just kids. But he was very troubled. He was angry—his parents were going through an acrimonious divorce, they were always on the edge financially, and he still resented their decision to move away from the small town where he'd grown up, in the foothills of the Oregon Cascades.

Most distressing, though, was his indecision about whether our relationship was over or not. Some days, yes—others, maybe not. It seemed to be a matter of convenience. But I'd been taught loyalty and persistence. When I questioned him, the anger surfaced—not to the extent that I felt threatened, but enough to make me feel rotten. I knew I should get out of the relationship. But I had trouble doing so, and the thing limped along. *What was I thinking?* I still asked myself.

I also longed to leave the suburban community where I'd grown up. I'd always felt miscast there and much preferred the city. I loved Seattle and frequently took the bus downtown to wander through the Pike Place Market and the odd collection of businesses along First Avenue. In the late 70s, that part of downtown was hardly gentrified; it comprised a moth-eaten string of pawn shops, a donut shop, and several Army-Navy surplus stores. I frequented the pawn shops, where I dreamt of discovering an old French horn—the instrument I still play—for sale inexpensively, one that restoration would reveal to be a treasure.

As the deadline neared for deciding whether to accept Scripps's offer of admission, I procrastinated. And I made what I can only describe in retrospect as an evasive maneuver—I said neither "yes" nor "no." Instead, I signed up for a room in a UW residence hall and proceeded on autopilot.

In Death Valley, I continued timing fish copulations. Their numbers seemed to be expanding; fish darted about with astonishing speed, in a pattern much like the geometric lines of a cat's cradle. Visually tracking their crazy and seemingly random movement was beginning to make me dizzy. The raw, white desert light spilled down in torrents, and the air hummed with heat. I could smell the sun-heated rocks surrounding the pool, where lizards were sunning themselves. I'd begun to feel a little lightheaded when a loud voice came from just behind me.

"Hey, Crowder, how's it going? Got some hot action in that pool?"

Startled, I jumped and turned to find Wendy, grinning from beneath an oversized straw hat with a floppy brim, her long, dark hair pulled back in a careless ponytail. Her nose was covered liberally in zinc oxide, the stark white giving her the aspect of a goofy hippie clown.

Wendy was the reason I was there that day. A freshman science major, she'd come sauntering through the hallway of our residence hall the night before, trolling for volunteers on behalf of one of her professors, the study director. She'd told me it would be an all-day trip, with an early departure—Death Valley was a four-hour drive away. But I hadn't hesitated to say yes. The study sounded interesting, and I'd liked Wendy immediately—she was friendly and open, with an easygoing and unselfconscious manner that seemed to epitomize the laid-back Southern California sensibility.

"Death Valley?" I'd asked, intrigued. "Fish in solar pools?" Beyond a lot of homework, I'd had nothing planned and the expedition sounded weird enough to be fun. Plus, my mother was a middle-school earth sciences teacher who made every family outing or camping trip an educational opportunity. She'd have jumped at this chance. If nothing else, I had to do it for her.

"Sure—sounds cool!" I'd told Wendy. "Just tell me when and where."

Throughout the preceding spring, in the months before my high school graduation, I'd continued managing to avoid the subject of Scripps and the fast-approaching enrollment deadline. But a letter from the admissions office reminded my parents, who made it clear I could sit on the fence no longer. The letter described a program designed to introduce prospective students to the college. My mom was enthusiastic.

"This looks like an excellent opportunity. You attend a couple of classes on Friday, then spend a weekend in a residence hall as the guest of a student before flying home Monday."

It would, she pointed out, give me a more tangible, concrete idea of the college. "You'd be making your choice from a more informed perspective."

Why not? I remember thinking. *No harm in visiting.*

So my dad made airline reservations and within a few days I was at the airport with my parents, waiting at the departure gate. When my flight began boarding, my dad handed me a check made out to Scripps for the commitment fee. As I took it, he said, "On Monday, before leaving Claremont, either give this to the Scripps admissions office or bring it back to me. But it's your decision; don't call us. You can tell us what you decided when we pick you up."

Those words didn't seem remarkable at the time, though I was a little surprised at hearing "Don't call us." It didn't take me long, though, to realize what an extraordinary gesture this had been. My parents knew me well, and trusted me to make the right decision. I imagine it took a lot of courage to withhold themselves from the process. I still think of it as the best thing they ever did for me. They set me free.

My stay at Scripps far exceeded any expectations I'd had. The classes I'd attended that Friday were all small seminars, where students and professors engaged in lively and intelligent discussion. All the women I met were interesting, well read, and cultured—yet still genuine and unassuming. And the campus, with its Mediterranean-style architecture and park-like grounds, was the most beautiful I'd ever seen. When I met my parents at the flight's arrival gate the following Monday, I immediately announced, "I'm going to Scripps." They were delighted, and quickly cancelled the arrangements for the UW dorm. I felt no trace of indecision; I had never been so certain of making the right choice.

At the edge of the pool, Wendy relieved me of my stopwatch and wilting page of stats and handed me a cold can of Coke. "We're done," she said. "Everyone's toasted and my prof says we have enough data. Time to head back to Claremont. First, drink the Coke. There's more in the truck. You're looking a little peaked, and we can't have anyone getting heatstroke."

Never a cola fan, I was grateful for this can. I popped open the top and drank deeply. It was a glorious moment when the wall of cold, sweet liquid hit the back of my throat. I realized how desperately thirsty I'd become, and gulped down the entire can within seconds.

We returned to the group assembled in a dusty parking lot around our pickup and two college minivans. Everyone was hot, tired, and sunburned.

As Wendy opened the cab's passenger door, she yelped as she touched the metal door handle. A wave of intense heat rushed out the open door.

"Yow! The metal's hotter than hell. And it's an oven in there."

Conor gingerly touched the side of the truck.

"Yeah, that's vicious. I was going to suggest you two ride in the back of the truck since it'll be breezy. But we've got to cool the bed first. You're in luck…this problem's not new."

The truck's contents included two buckets, which Conor carried to a water spigot I hadn't noticed. Apparently this wasn't just a parking lot, but a nominal rest area.

Water rushed from the spigot. "Deep well; the water's pretty cold," Conor remarked, filling the buckets and then upending them into the truck bed. He repeated this, gauging the metal's temperature with his palm until finally pronouncing the bed fit for occupancy.

"Better a wet ass than a scalded one," he drawled as we climbed in, before closing the tailgate.

The next hour passed in a dreamlike blur of heat, light, and rushing wind. At first it was uncomfortable, with the truck bouncing along the rutted, unpaved access road. But soon we reached the smooth pavement of the highway. The desert scenery streamed past—mostly rocks and sand, with an occasional sagebrush, mesquite, or stand of furry-limbed *cholla* cactus. Tumbleweeds nearly as high as the truck skipped along ahead of the wind, shattering when we hit them. In the background, the distant mountains appeared to float above a band of afternoon haze.

It was all so new, so foreign. It occurred to me that I'd given practically no thought to my former boyfriend since the start of the semester. Unexpectedly, I hadn't been homesick, either. I was making a lot of friends. Best of all, no one here knew me; I had no history. And that was tremendously liberating.

After lunch at a truck stop, we learned that one last activity remained in the day. We'd passed through several tiny, no-name towns, which Wendy said were populated largely by "desert rats"—longtime desert residents who were as brown, wrinkled, and thirsty-looking as their surroundings. At one of these towns, Conor abruptly turned into a parking lot, stopping in front of a low building with a sign proclaiming: **Spa**. It seemed odd, but by then I was too tired to ask questions.

Getting out of the truck, Conor's only remark was, "Can't return to Claremont looking like the great unwashed."

The spa's special attraction soon became evident. It was segregated by sex, women and men each having their own set of thermal pools. And everyone was naked. Two aged women smiled as they passed us, heading toward the pools, free of clothes and any hint of apology for their wrinkled, sagging skin.

Wendy turned to me, grinning. "Well. This is, shall we say, *unique*."

I nodded. "I think you're right. It appears we've found the desert rat's native…habitat."

We snickered nervously. Wendy paused, and then said, "If it helps, I'm sure you don't have any parts I haven't seen elsewhere."

We stripped and went in.

We tried three pools before settling in the coolest of them with a group of locals. When Wendy briefly left the pool to get fresh bottles of water, one woman loudly exclaimed, observing her return, "Oh, now, isn't it nice to see some firm young flesh for a change?"

Wendy, chagrined, ducked quickly back into the water while the other residents of the pool cackled their assent. But they were kind women, if a little nutty. They were curious about where we were from and what we were doing there, and an animated conversation ensued. When we finally left, it felt as if we'd acquired a whole new set of grandmothers.

What was it about that day in Death Valley that made it so magical and resonant in my memory? I believe it marked a turning point, the moment when I recognized what a completely new and radically different place this was—one where I was free to transform myself into the person I wanted to be. It was the right "ecosystem" for me at the time.

By insisting that I make the decision about school independently, my parents gave me the freedom to choose—and to leave. Many risks followed that one, creating a set of experiences that helped me develop strength I hadn't known myself to be capable of. The person I became would not again, for example, seek anyone's approval at the expense of self-respect and integrity, or hesitate to leave an unsatisfying relationship.

The time I spent in Claremont was transformative. I learned as much inside as outside my classes—from my professors to the women in the desert spa alike. Those four years made vivid and real the Scripps motto, "Incipit Vita Nova," from Dante—"Here begins a new life."

MAMA AND HER LIQUOR LICENSE
By Eleanor Owen

MAMA WAS HEADSTRONG AND AHEAD OF HER TIME. In the early 1900s, at age seventeen, she emigrated from Italy determined to "stand on her own two feet and make something of herself." Despite having little education, she was profoundly wise, fiercely independent, and interested only in matters of importance. We, her eight kids, knew we were important, and what we did mattered. Each day, her solid frame hovered over us as we lined up at the door on our way to school. Standing firm, she emptied a slimy spoonful of smelly cod liver oil into our open mouths, then dropped in a segment of tangerine or a sliver of tart apple, followed by a warning: "Do nothing to make your mother ashamed."

On her invisible slate—where she kept score on everything we did or didn't do—I was certain that, either above or just below cod liver oil, leafy vegetables, and clean school clothes, she had scribbled *Education*. She often reminded us, "Within a month after stepping off Ellis Island I signed up for night school." Her goal was to speak English without an Italian accent. It was one of the few goals that she and Papa, also an immigrant, held in common. Mama always nodded in approval when she heard Papa stop relatives from uttering a word of Italian in our home, and say.

"I don't want my boys to be ditch diggers or my girls to work in factories. They need to learn how to speak like a lawyer, so they can become Supreme Court Judges."

His lectures would prompt me to study the newspaper clipping of the nine Supreme Court Judges he kept nailed to a wall in his garage.

I used to imagine how all eight of us, plus one of my cousins, would pose in those nun's dresses when we became the Judges. However, unlike in the picture, as the eldest girl in the family I would make sure we buttoned them closed.

Mama had a broader view. Being Catholic, she was equally concerned with our souls. She said teachers gave us many lessons to learn in school, so she gave us only three. We heard them often, and were expected to obey without question:

1. Never steal. Not a penny, not a ten-dollar bill, not a diamond bracelet. Nothing. Never.

2. Always tell the truth. The whole truth. Everything. Always.

3. Stay a virgin until you marry.

These rules were cast in stone, and, pretty much, she got her way. Not one hundred percent, but pretty close. As for doing what we pleased, that seemed to work out OK, too. Individually and collectively, we learned to take risks and accept the consequences, to draw the line for ourselves, and to speak up without fear. And nobody ever went to prison.

Aside from her three rules, Mama fostered independence on a regular basis. And she never interfered with whatever we did, especially, she said, when it was "to learn something new."

Once, she let me slash into a silvery lace bureau scarf to embellish the bodice of a prom dress I was making for my sister Gloria. She watched me take scissors to the delicate metallic scarf, and coached, "Make it like Schiaparelli." Then she added, "But better." This gift stunned me because I once overheard her confide to Giulia, her best friend, that when she boarded the ship in Naples and set sail for America, the hand embroidered scarf and her virginity were the only two things she brought as her trousseau.

Such indulgences came naturally to Mama. They seemed like embraces from her own outrageous pride, as well as from her unwavering conviction that we kids were born fully equipped to chart our own lives, and that by obeying her three rules, we were "destined to always hold our heads high and make it into heaven." What we didn't know was that she was including herself in that vision, planning her own future.

In addition to the vigilance she kept regarding her rules, Mama was constantly alert for other opportunities to keep us on course in our earthly life. And not just us kids; she doled out advice with ease and authority to anyone she felt needed to learn a lesson or two. There was, however, one major difference: Inside our home, if you failed to change your school clothes or left the water running in the sink, or started a fight, she was quick with a smack on the back of your head or a hard pinch anywhere she could grab; outside the home, Mama believed her children could do no wrong.

One time, Miss Whitaker, a flat, angular spinster who taught the upper grades in the three-room schoolhouse in upstate New York, mailed a letter complaining about my "deportment." Mama snorted at the word. She re-read the letter and puffed, "Deportment—is she thinking of sending you to Italy?"

When I saw Mama draw up one side of her mouth and squint, I recognized a look that meant Miss Whitaker was about to be given a lesson. Mama muttered, mostly to herself, "It can't be important. Hmmm. She hasn't learned that small words like *sin* or *spit* carry more weight than big ones." The whole while she darted penetrating looks that questioned whether I had done either or both. Having heard how Mama once told Mildred's second-grade teacher that she would "mop the floor with her if she ever struck one of her children again," I dreaded the lesson Mama might be planning for Miss Whitaker.

At the scheduled meeting, Mama arrived wearing a church dress and her thick, black hair roped into a neat, shiny bun. She looked impatient, as though she had been taken away from more important business. When Miss Whitaker complained that I was always interrupting and blurting out answers—even to questions for the seventh and eighth-grade rows—without raising my hand or being granted permission, Mama raised her chin a notch higher, then carefully explained, acting like a supervisor, "Well, that's her way of telling you she's learned that lesson. You need to give her harder work to do." She waited, and, getting no response, added, "From the higher row."

They stared at each other for a few moments. When Miss Whitaker dropped her gaze first, Mama, looking like the problem had been resolved to her satisfaction, considered the matter closed, and, to my relief, got up to leave. At the door, she turned and, *very* politely, said, "It's good that you pay such close attention to the children." Miss Whitaker looked confused, not sure if this was meant as a compliment or reprimand. I thought, *Exactly the lesson Mama intended.*

One spring, decades later, my siblings and I were in store for yet another lesson from Mama. It began when I received a phone call from my sister Gloria, urging me to come east for a visit. "Something important is going on with Mama. Men with pads and rulers are coming and going around the fruit stand."

The fruit stand was a sturdy wooden structure Mama bought for twenty-five dollars from Pine Tree Inn when it closed its golf course during the depths of the Great Depression. She paid a local farmer two dollars to haul it down the road and place it on our property along the 9W highway in upstate New York. I recall how she stood back, visibly pleased, and said, "Kids, now you can begin to sell fruit from our orchard and learn how to make a penny for yourselves,"

Gloria, born with an instinct to organize, coaxed, "Gen and Leo will be coming up from Florida. If you come, we can all spend Easter dinner with Mama." She had no details, but there was an urgency in her voice that caused me to wonder. *Perhaps, now that we were all grown with families of our own, had Zia Marietta, Mama's older sister, who had visited a year earlier, talked Mama into selling the farm and returning to Italy to live with her? Was Mama sick and secretly putting her house in order? Had she run out of money?* Something was in the air.

I was further convinced this family get-together was really important when Gloria asked my sister Evelyn, who lived near Mama, to phone on Palm Sunday and confirm everyone's attendance. I flew from the West Coast, Genevieve came from Florida, and my brothers and their families drove upstate from Staten Island and Brooklyn.

We celebrated Easter Sunday with everyone home for a huge family gathering. Nieces and nephews ate at the large kitchen table, three dogs ran helter-skelter in and out of the house, in-laws looked awkward and out of place, and parents yelled at their children for sneaking cannoli from the pink boxes filled with pastry that Francey bought at Alfonso's on Staten Island..

At our big dining table, early talk compared the eggplant Parmigiano with last year's, everyone raved about Genevieve's ravioli, and the splash of brandy in the zabaglione made it more fragrant and better than ever. Gloria was praised for sending a load of ripe Concord grapes to Francey, and he was praised for making the wine. Tasting, testing, and talking about food was the way our family dinners always started.

Finally, nonchalantly, Mama announced, "I'm going to open a restaurant."

We gasped in unison; shouts followed. Alarmed, a couple of nieces ran into the dining room and stood next to their parents. Everyone talked at the same time, each demanding to be heard. Rose, my gentle sister-in-law, whispered, "You're sixty!"

"Yes, sixty," several of us chorused, almost as one. One niece questioned,

"Sixty?"

"So? Someday you'll be sixty. Want to sit around doing nothing?"

"Where will it be? You can't convert the barn," Mildred said, barely concealing her anxiety over the truckload of antiques she had kept stored there for years. Mama stiffened her back and lifted her head; her dark eyes glistened.

"I'm adding on to the fruit stand. Making a real building. With bricks."

Our response was total, collective silence. Taking advantage of the pause, Mama, growing bolder by the second, carried on, "The workers are starting tomorrow."

Amid an explosion of louder moans, I thought, *If she is determined to do this, she has picked a good spot. It's on the main highway to Albany, the state capitol, not too far from town, and fairly close to West Point.*

The objections and pleas continued. Nobody listened to anybody. Only Albert, Mama's favorite son, whom she called her "Ruby," and who was well on his way to becoming a multimillionaire (having parlayed the small reserves from Papa's trucking business into investments as a slum landlord), sat quietly or guffawed at the rantings, periodically mocking or mimicking our futile efforts. While arguments swelled, he tipped back on his chair, smirking.

Following Papa's death, Albert had seen to it that Mama wanted for nothing. I suspected that he probably knew of Mama's plans and already had decided to absorb the costs as quasi-legal business write-offs.

Snatches of sentences bounced around: "time to slow down ... we'll come to eat more often ... young hoodlums will rob you ... you've never even worked in a restaurant ... don't know what's involved ... who's going to keep books? ... what books? ... the brook's too close and a kid will fall in ... you'll get sued ... no more junking at yard sales ... no more naps ... "

Francey, the eldest, had been quiet throughout. Now he warned, "You'll have to get a liquor license and serve anybody who walks in and wants a drink." He knew Mama loathed drunks.

"I'll never get a liquor license," Mama scoffed. Her raised eyebrows and the snap of her head told him that he was beginning to drink too much himself.

"How can you have an Italian meal without wine?" my brother-in-law Jeff gently taunted. *ZING*, I thought, *that'll do it*.

But Mama didn't budge. She sat there, looking regal, taking it all in, her lips sealed and her eyes and hands preoccupied with folding her napkin into smaller and smaller rectangles, each tighter than the last. Mama's plan, I realized, was non-negotiable.

The builders came and went, a big stove and refrigerator were installed, and lovely white tablecloths covered odd-shaped tables. Mama had special shelves built to show off her collection of ironstone pitchers, earthenware jugs, glazed Deruta pottery, and Meissen vases. She coaxed me into making fancy curtains with "scalloped edges" and beamed at her creation. It was old-fashioned Italian, like in her native land, complete with an assortment of napkins that she had been collecting at estate sales for years. "Linen napkins," she boasted, "add a touch of quality."

The décor was truly charming. Mildred called it "eclectic." The dishes, flatware, platters, and glasses came from years of rummaging at garage sales. Nothing matched. At the same table one diner might be eating from an early Peter Max plate, another from a delicate hand-painted French Limoges, and two others from dishes that did match but were different sizes. Glasses ranged from oddly shaped Sears and Roebuck goblets to elegant footed Venetian Crystal. She even moved the life-sized Carrara marble statue of a Victorian child from our home's vestibule into the restaurant's entryway.

Mama hired two helpers, notified her nearby grandchildren that she might need them from time to time, and she was on her way. Within two months, she became the darling of West Point cadets who brought girlfriends or parents from out of town. As they stepped inside, the sweet scent of roasted red peppers or the steamy, fresh pasta "gravy" slowly simmering on the back burner lured them farther in. The "regulars" often poked their heads into the kitchen, where Mama might give them a spoon to lick or a chunk of cheese to nibble on.

The restaurant was always busy. She hired additional help to clean up at the end of the day, and Mildred asked her friend, Sadie, an art teacher, to make a hand-scripted sign tastefully decorated in Italy's red, white, and green. Posted near the entrance, it read "Mama DeVito's Italian Kitchen."

"How is she doing?" I asked when Mildred phoned cross-country to give me an update.

"Great. It's unbelievable. She gets personal with everyone and treats customers like family. They all call her Mama. She even keeps dough in the fridge and invites the fidgety kids into the kitchen to roll out their own pasta."

Treating everyone like family also meant that Mama exposed her audacious streak. Shortly after serving the main dish, she would approach each table and talk about the handpicked, tender dandelion leaves she had added to their salad, or share her recipe for broiled clams with rosemary and garlic. If a diner asked for a recipe, she invited her into the kitchen. "The only way to learn is to watch me make it," she'd say.

She might ask a young child if he had started school and tease his adolescent sister by questioning, "Are boys beginning to hang around?" If this were a second or third visit for the family, she would wink at the girl and, placing emphasis to make her point, advise her to "Watch your pussy. Save your cherry for your husband. Then you'll always be the boss." She would laugh softly, delighted at the reactions of awe, surprise or embarrassment, and, keeping eye contact with the young girl, she would nod her head like a sage.

Inevitably, she would end the conversation by suggesting that the diners come back on Thursdays to taste her homemade potato gnocchi. Secretly, she was assessing the mood and type of customers at the tables before returning to the kitchen. Once there, she would select exactly the right size pitcher from her hoard and fill it with red wine—an amount *she* determined to be *just enough*. Mama would remove her apron, emerge from the kitchen, go to the diners, smile, set the pitcher down before the person who she believed would pick up the bill, and beam. "Taste. Taste. My son makes this wine. I get it free. No charge."

Mama's reputation spread.

Two state troopers came regularly on Thursdays with their families. They received generous portions of the gnocchi and slightly larger pitchers than others. If, however, a diner had been drinking beforehand and seemed to be getting high and asked for a "refill," she would smile, showing her beautiful teeth, and say (sounding overly apologetic), "I'm sorry, the gallon's empty. Sorry. My son will bring more next week. Come back."

Mama continued in this way until two months before she died, on her birthday, at age ninety-seven.

And she never got a liquor license.

PROBABILITIES OF LOVE AND CANCER

By Christiane Banta

WHEN I TOLD MY GRANDMOTHER I'D BEEN DIAGNOSED with breast cancer, she gave me this advice: "Do just what your doctor tells you."

She wasn't the only one to give me advice. I was inundated, overwhelmed, and buried by directions from people who knew me—and people who didn't—on how to be a savvy cancer patient. I was given advice on every aspect of my life, from taking up yoga to never accepting anything a doctor said without getting a second opinion.

I tried. I took yoga classes, met with a hypnotherapist, and joined a support group, even though by nature I'm not a joiner. I talked to the friends of friends who had gone through treatments. I read books and waded through online resources. But I lost interest very quickly. I'd just started dating Jim, a guy I had known for a long time, and it felt right—and thinking about him was definitely more interesting than doing research on cancer and its treatments.

We're all familiar with denial, but the weird thing about it is how logical and real it feels when we're living there. I'm an actuary. I work with probabilities, and I understand statistics. So I looked at the probabilities of cancer, and chances were much better that I didn't have cancer than that I did. So in the beginning, I was sure my abnormal mammogram wasn't cancer, but in fact, it was. Then, I was sure the cancer would be early-stage and easily treated, but it wasn't. Then, I was sure that whatever I went through, I would be able to handle it, and when it was over I'd be cancer-free. As far as I can tell, I did get that one right, at least.

After I had my abnormal but inconclusive mammogram, I was randomly assigned to Dr. Song, a surgeon who specialized in breast cancer treatments. When she told me I had breast cancer, I started to cry, which I'm sure is not unusual for her patients. But I wasn't crying because I had cancer, I was crying because I didn't understand. The mammogram was inconclusive, so how could Dr. Song come to a conclusion? That's the actuary in me: I take things literally.

Dr. Song scheduled a biopsy to confirm her diagnosis, or, as she said, "Because you didn't believe me." I didn't know what to say to her when she said that because *belief* seemed so irrelevant. But instead of telling her I needed her to explain what was going on in a way I could understand, I just cried.

Three days after Dr. Song's diagnosis, I had my first real date with Jim. I'd known Jim for over 10 years because he was also an actuary, and we'd worked at the same company. I had hardly seen him in the last three years since I'd moved from Seattle to take a job in California. I visited Seattle every month, however, and on one visit I called him and suggested we have lunch. After a few friendly lunches, during which we reestablished our earlier easy rapport, we made plans for dinner and a movie. It was pretty clear this was going to be the day the friendship would become a romance. And that's exactly what happened.

Of course, I had to tell Jim about Dr. Song's diagnosis, even though by then I had convinced myself that she was wrong and I didn't really have cancer. Jim kissed me for the first time and told me he wanted to be with me whatever happened.

My biopsy appointment was scheduled for so early in the morning that the hospital wasn't even open. I walked through the dark halls and past empty reception desks and waiting rooms to get to the Radiology Department. I worried that I'd misunderstood my instructions. I read and reread them as I waited in the dark hallway outside Room 5.

Finally, the door opened and a woman stepped out into the hall.

"Good morning," she said. "I'm Kathleen, and I'll be helping with your biopsy this morning." Kathleen was the technologist who had given me my mammogram. Afterwards, she had looked at me with such sympathy that it had scared me. Then I got angry at her for scaring me for what I thought was nothing.

"We've already met," I said. "You did my mammogram a couple of weeks ago."

She looked puzzled. She still didn't remember me. I realized she saw dozens of people every day, but I thought she would remember that look as much as I did. I guess I was just one more cancer patient to her. Kathleen prepared me for the radiologist, helping me recline on a bed in the ultrasound room, covered only by a paper gown above my waist.

Then, the most beautiful woman I had ever seen entered the room. Dr. Kimura had a very soft kind of beauty, her round face and wide, green eyes framed by smooth, dark-brown hair that fell loosely past her flawless skin to her shoulders. She moved gracefully and noiselessly around the room, somehow seeming both competent and compassionate. I liked her immediately and felt complete confidence in her ability. I also recognized how shallow I was being. I felt confidence in her only because of her looks and manner—okay, *mostly* because of her looks.

Dr. Kimura gave me a local anesthesia, then cut a small opening in my skin, inserted a needle, and captured a sample, using ultrasound to guide her path.

"Do you feel any pain?" she asked.

"No," I said. I really didn't feel any pain, and was just feeling glad that she had finally said something to me. I wanted to keep talking to her but couldn't think of anything to say.

I was surprised when she inserted a second needle and captured another sample. I had been told about the biopsy procedure, but not that more than one needle would be used.

Dr. Kimura now held a third needle, but she paused before using it. Her brow furrowed.

"I'm sorry," she said. I looked up at her, knowing I would forgive her anything. "I always tell the patient what to expect before I start, and I forgot to tell you."

"Oh, that's okay," I said. I thought about telling her I was just thinking about that, but I was afraid she would think I was criticizing her. I wanted her to feel like we had really connected. Maybe she would tell her friends and colleagues what an amazing patient I was. But then I realized it was much more likely she would forget me, the way Kathleen had.

Dr. Kimura took several more samples, and then told me she was done.

"You have a very high pain threshold," she told me with a lovely smile that lit up her eyes. I smiled back, but I felt uneasy. No one had told me what she was doing might have hurt.

Kathleen bandaged my breast and gave me a couple of small, round, cold packs about the size of bathtub drain plugs. She instructed me to put them in the freezer, and, when they were cold, to put them on the incision sites to control the swelling.

I went home and called Jim.

"I'm sitting on the couch topless, with an ice cube on my breast," I told him.

"Oooooooooh," he said. Then he paused. "I guess that's probably not a good thing, huh?"

"It's okay," I said. "I don't feel any pain, I was just told to do this to keep the swelling down."

"*Swelling*," he said, then made a hungry growling sound. I laughed.

"Call me when you get the results," he said.

"I will," I promised.

Late the next afternoon—a Friday—Dr. Song called me. I was still at work.

"I knew you would want to hear as soon as possible," she said.

I wasn't so sure I did, actually. I had planned to have a pleasant weekend, not thinking about the test. I wasn't anxious because I pretty much figured the results were going to be negative. That was the most probable outcome. But there she was on the phone, so I told her to go ahead.

It was bad news. It was definitely cancer, a fast-growing, aggressive type. Treatments weren't going to be easy. She recommended throwing everything they could at the cancer. She said I was only 42, I was strong, I would recover my health. Dr. Song talked and talked as I listened, stunned. I couldn't think of anything to say. Eventually, we hung up.

I collapsed on the floor of my office, sobbing. My office wasn't soundproof—it was really just a cubicle with a door and walls that went up to the ceiling. Everyone passed my office to leave the building and must have heard my loud crying. I was embarrassed and wanted to leave, but I couldn't even stand up. It took a half an hour before

I was able to stop crying long enough to get out of the building and into my car.

I didn't call Jim immediately. I couldn't figure out what to say to him, and I was afraid I would just cry. But I knew he would want to know I had the results early, so I emailed him and said I had the results but wouldn't be able to talk to him about it until later. Of course, he knew that meant it was bad news.

By the time we talked that weekend, I had regained my optimism. I now accepted that I had cancer—a scary, fast-growing cancer—but I'd convinced myself it had probably been found in the early stages. I'd decided I would have a short, but not-too-difficult treatment. I explained the probabilities to Jim and he agreed with me. Then we talked about other, more pleasant things.

After a couple of hours my ear was getting tired, so I moved the phone receiver around to my other ear. As the phone left one ear, I heard Jim say, "I–" and as it came within hearing of my other ear, I heard, "you." His low tone of voice made me think he had just said "I love you," but what if he hadn't? We had only been going out a couple of weeks, so I hadn't expected we would say we loved each other yet. If I said, "I love you, too," and he had actually said, "I miss you," that would be embarrassing.

"What?" I said.

"What?" he answered. He thought I was teasing him.

"No, no. Honestly, I didn't hear you. What did you say?"

"What did I say?"

I was beginning to panic. His coyness convinced me that he had said he loved me. What if he didn't say it again for a while? Did he regret having said it?

"Jim, seriously. I was moving the phone to my other ear, and I missed what you said. I heard 'I' and 'you' but not what you said in between."

"I said 'I love you,'" he said.

Whew! What a relief.

"I love you, too," I said. "Of course, you know that, as I know that you love me. But it's nice to hear." *I should have stopped with "I love you,"* I thought. *Everything else I said was kind of incoherent.*

It was the moment when we first said we loved each other, and I'd blown it. I was happy that we'd said it, but disappointed that it had turned into such a comedy routine. I decided that when I told others the story, I wouldn't reveal that the first time Jim had said he loved me, I hadn't heard him. I would say, "He said it first."

Dr. Song called me the next week to talk about scheduling chemotherapy. As she talked, tears slowly trickled down my cheek. I told her I didn't want to have chemotherapy first, as she had recommended. A definitive diagnosis wasn't possible until after surgery, and I was expecting my diagnosis would confirm that what I had was actually early-stage cancer, with no need for chemotherapy. She told me that wasn't going to happen, that chemotherapy would be necessary. My tears became a stream. I couldn't understand why she was so certain, and, as usual, I didn't know how to ask her. I told her I would think about what she said and hung up.

I went to another doctor for a second opinion and got all the explanations I had wanted. I knew I had to leave Dr. Song, even though she was one of the best breast cancer doctors at the hospital, because every time she talked to me I cried, and then I couldn't get the information I needed from her. So I decided to have the treatment that Dr. Song recommended, but with the other doctor.

I saw Dr. Kimura again two weeks after the phone call with Dr. Song. I hadn't expected to see her that day. I had an appointment in Radiology to place a metal chip in my breast next to the tumor, and she was the doctor who showed up. The chip would mark where the tumor used to be if chemotherapy shrunk the tumor to nothing.

When Dr. Kimura opened the door and came in, I smiled. Again I was struck by her soft loveliness, and also thought how silly I was to respond to her only because of the way she looked.

"Dr. Kimura!" I said, the delight obvious in my voice. She gave me a small smile. I wondered if she actually remembered me.

"These aren't the right kind of needle, but I don't want to ask you to come back, so I'll try to get one of these to work," she said, holding up a box.

I felt like a teenager, thrilled that the most popular girl in school had asked me to join her for lunch. I had her attention for a short time. Maybe I could get her to like me.

"The procedure won't take long and shouldn't be painful," she said. "Maybe I can use just a surface numbing rather than deep anesthesia."

"You said before that I had a high pain threshold," I said. She smiled at me again, but not as if she remembered what I was talking about.

She cut a small slit in my skin and pushed in the needle and chip. I could tell she was struggling to get the needle in straight; she kept pulling it back and then pushing again. Finally she gave up.

"I'm sorry," she said. "This needle just isn't going to work. I didn't want to ask you to come back, but I'm going to have to."

As she cleaned the incision point and bandaged it, Dr. Kimura chatted with me. I suspected she was rewarding me for being a good patient. I was going to take advantage of this.

I'd been thinking about all the medical professionals I would be working with during my months of treatments. I was only one of many patients they saw, so they would probably forget me between appointments, as Kathleen had. I wondered if difficult patients might actually get better care than well-behaved patients just because they got the doctors' attention. I didn't want to be a difficult patient, but what if good patients weren't memorable? I had decided then that I would connect with my doctors by telling them a story they didn't hear every day; I would tell them about Jim and my brand-new relationship. I planned to be shameless, to milk our story at every opportunity. I would try to get my doctors invested in my happy ending.

"We actually started going out the same week I was diagnosed," I told Dr. Kimura. "I told him about the cancer and he said he wanted to go through it with me. He told me he loves me already." I let my face show her how happy I was. I bet she didn't see happiness on her patients' faces very often.

I returned to the hospital two days later, and Dr. Kimura quickly and efficiently placed the chip in my breast. Her manner was completely detached, focused on her medical responsibilities. I stayed silent as she worked. After bandaging the incision point, Dr. Kimura walked to the door, ready to leave. Before opening the door, she turned back and looked at me.

"How are things with your boyfriend?" she asked. "His name is Jim, right?"

"Things are great," I said. "He's coming here next Monday, to be with me for my first chemotherapy treatment."

She smiled at me, then opened the door and left. I felt triumphant. She remembered me.

I would see Dr. Kimura again months later, the day of my surgery, and she still remembered me and asked about Jim. After my success with her, I had told everyone about Jim and my relationship, and it seemed to work. Most of the doctors remembered me and asked about Jim when he wasn't with me. One doctor even asked me for advice on her own long-distance relationship.

So in the end, my grandmother was *sort of* right. I had to trust that the doctors had the training they needed to do a good job. But I didn't have to be passive. I could get their attention, and maybe even make them care about me. And I could make sure I had a doctor that I could get answers from, so that I could understand what was going to happen.

As he had promised, Jim was with me through everything—in person when he could be there, and in spirit when he couldn't. I don't know what the probability is that a relationship that starts with cancer treatments will succeed, but ours has continued to be very successful. Even more improbably, those months were among the happiest of my life.

LESSONS STILL LEARNING: I ONCE WAS LOST BUT NOW I'M FOUND

By Peggy A. Nagae

In a recent conversation with my friend Robin, I was surprised to find myself thinking out loud about Charlie, my ex-husband, in a neutral manner with no attachment to him. At the time we separated—over eight years ago now—I could barely function, had problems focusing on work, and thought about him and the woman he left me for, nonstop. Another friend, Barbara, put a name to my feelings.

She said, "Your heart is broken."

I responded, "So this is what a broken heart feels like. I had no idea."

I had no idea, even though I'd been divorced before and boyfriends had broken up with me. This was different because I not only totally trusted him—I was totally committed to our marriage.

A part of me felt that big rockets should have exploded or an array of fireworks should have lit up the Montana sky the moment my heart was healed or when I finally got over Charlie, but that was not the case. Instead, these changes took place without my conscious awareness, maybe more like a metamorphosis than a cataclysmic event.

Charlie had been my elixir, my third husband, the one about whom I thought, "This is it! The third time *is* the charm." I finally committed to "till death do us part." Truthfully, I also thought our marriage would work because I was a good catch for him: heart-centered and professional, financially independent, spiritual and committed. I thought he would love me, even adore me, and be grateful to be married to me, all things I craved in a relationship. I also thought he was my heart's choice: a spiritual man who believed in the human potential movement, and willing to "go the distance" for our relationship. We vowed we would tell each other the microscopic truth; we worked with a relationship coach before we got married just to "make sure." Maybe that's why I was so stunned when I found out about his affair with Norine, a friend of mine from my spiritual class.

Sad memories about the affair remained, and I did still feel he'd lacked the courage and integrity to come clean and tell me of the affair before I upended my life in Oregon, and yet suddenly, those memories no longer held the same charge for me. Somehow, all had shifted.

Looking back, our relationship had been good for many years. We bought and sold several houses, remodeling them together. I would add my ideas, but Charlie's artistic sensibilities, carpentry skills, and technological knowledge made our remodeling projects easier, more creative, and less expensive than if we'd had contractors do all the work. He re-wired, laid floating wood floors, lowered ceilings, and updated bathrooms.

On weekends, we did errands together and had fun doing them. Also, Charlie served as the IT expert for my business, and took care of "manly things" like the cars and garbage, upkeep of the house, and mowing the lawn. Charlie did the bulk of the household chores while I earned the bulk of our income. After selling the herbal products' business in which he'd been a minority owner, he said he was burned out, tired of corporate life, and didn't want to return to that rat race. He wanted to take time off and maybe attend art classes. I wanted to support his desires, especially since his parents had not done so earlier in his life. So being a supportive partner, I said I would continue working while he took time off.

He attended art school and created amazing artwork. The school selected his bronze piece for a national competition. He also took care of many other chores: paying bills, cooking, driving our girls to their activities, and even helping me pack for my business trips. No matter the time of day, he would drive me to the airport and pick me up when I returned.

We also did sweet things for each other: wrote love notes, sent cards, and talked every night when I worked out of town. We bought each other wonderful presents for holidays, birthdays, and other special occasions. He was a great partner in other ways: he had sound advice about management and leadership. I had read a lot of management books; he had read none but had everyday experiences and lots of practical, emotional, and intuitive intelligences. We regularly discussed work-related issues or did things like brainstorming the entire outline for a book over the phone while he was on a motorcycle trip and I was in Seattle writing with my co-author.

We were a good team for much of our relationship, but somewhere, someplace, somehow, that shifted. We talked less and argued more. Even though I was the trial lawyer in the relationship, he himself was a fierce advocate. He would say I backed him into a corner and he had to defend himself, which he did quite well. I took to giving in, holding my tongue, managing myself, and being careful with our conversations. But even with the increased tension and stress, I felt our relationship would endure, given our marital commitments and spiritual growth courses. That's what took us to Montana several times a year—spiritual classes—and that was, in part, why we moved. We had friends there, a spiritual community. I was going to reduce my consulting practice, and we were going to hike together on a regular basis. Or that's what we said.

Our relationship got hard in bits and pieces: We stopped talking about fundamental issues; we disagreed but could not compromise; we "managed" our relationship; and, worst of all, we did not speak about how the relationship had changed. I made him wrong. I felt our relationship was not as intimate as it could be, and I wanted more sex. He wanted me to appreciate him more and stop being so demanding. We disagreed and were at odds with one another.

Even though we engaged in spiritual work, we did not work through our issues. We left them hanging. Our marriage now had jagged edges, and I wasn't sure how to soften them. I felt insecure, and worried about the marriage that I once thought was unflappable. I started acting insecure, tracking him during class, in meetings, and even at parties. I would know where he was in a crowd and with whom he was talking. I watched, tracked, and worried. Our intimacy tanked some more, and the relationship slipped another notch.

The more insecure I became, the more I wanted Charlie to demonstrate his love for me, tell me he loved me, and show his commitment by word and deed. I also wanted to talk through our issues and work them out. We did talk for hours, but all we did was go round and round, with no resolution, and without getting closer or more intimate. In short, we argued about issues without either of us hearing the other or shifting our positions. Each of us argued for being right.

I had thought the spiritual work complemented our relationship, but that is where he met Norine, my so-called friend. We were in the same spiritual class, which Charlie joined after September 11th. I thought it was lovely because it would be another aspect of our lives that we could share. Little did I know it would be our undoing: our spiritual work and classes served as the wellspring for their affair. Seems antithetical to fundamental spiritual principles, but there you have it.

I learned about his affair from email messages he had sent her. I confronted him about their affair, and he would not stop seeing her, so I asked him to move out. Shortly after that he began living with her. He got a job because he had to, unlike during our marriage. They lived in the same town and participated in the same social events, community meetings, and classes that I did.

For months, all I did was cry and feel raw, lost, and vulnerable. But even then, I hoped we could reconcile. I spent over a year open to that possibility before I realized it was not to be. I remember the exact day that the window of possibility for our marriage closed: July 16, 2005. I was sitting in a chapel at a memorial service. As I sat reflecting upon my friend's life, I realized that this was the end of hoping the world would change regarding Charlie and me. I also took stock, and it was not pretty: I was a fifty-something woman, left by her husband for a younger woman, feeling alone, betrayed, and kicked to the curb.

Many people have traveled the same path with similar pain. Many have found out about their partners' affairs. Many marriages have broken up; many hearts have been broken. I am not "the only one," but when it was happening to me, it felt like I was, like no one else could possibly understand the depth of my pain. No one else could comprehend either my sorrow or my humiliation.

My journey since has been a long and arduous one, filled with times of self-doubt, self-loathing, and self-pity, but also with self-reflection, self-love, and self-care. All these years later, I have my own life, wrought from the flames of that experience. It might sound dramatic, but that is exactly how I feel: I have been forged from the fires of my breakup with Charlie with life lessons forever etched in my soul.

On my journey, I took a long look at myself, my attitudes about men, and my role in relationships. Little by little, I guess I was changing—changing so much that finally I could think of Charlie as "just another person."

When Charlie and I split, I realized that I hadn't been alone since I was fourteen, and I began to ask myself why. It slowly became clear to me: I did not want to be alone and had been searching for someone to love me because if he did, then I would know I was okay. I wanted him to accept me, to pursue me, to show me I was loveable. I sought validation for being attractive, wanted, needed. I also looked for someone who would not leave me, someone safe. That's what I thought I had with Charlie: someone safe. We would stay together, and I would not have to be alone to face myself.

The pain of betrayal and abandonment was such a force when Charlie left that I finally said to myself, "Enough." Given my level of agony, I decided I would rather be alone than suffer more heartbreak. For the first time in my life, being alone was the better option. Slowly, I began to see that I used men so I did not have to deal with my insecurities. It began to dawn on me that whatever I sought from them, I needed to give to myself. If it is love I sought, then I needed to give myself love. If I needed them to make me feel beautiful, accepted, cherished, and adored, I needed to accept, cherish, and adore myself. There was no one who could give me enough love so that I would finally love myself. I was a bottomless pit of need, and no amount of anything from anyone would ever fill it. The filling-up is an inside job, my job, and not anyone else's.

So, even now, when I long to be part of a couple, I pull myself back and remind myself of self-love. When I want to feel valued or respected by others, I practice self-acceptance and self-validation. After years of focusing on what I need from others, I have gradually discovered what I can give myself. The critic in my head has quieted down, and another voice has begun to surface with kinder words about myself and for myself. That voice is stronger, and that is the voice of my soul.

For an entire year after our split, I kept everything in the house exactly as it had been. I realized, again, little by little, that I had to start taking care of all those things around the house that Charlie had tended. From changing light bulbs to taking out the trash, fixing stuck windows, mowing the lawn, or building stonewalls, he had done it all. I realized that I had gotten lazy about doing my share. He changed the oil in the cars, planted flowers and trees, landscaped the garden, and took care of the hot tub. He took the lawn chairs out and put them away in the fall, called the sprinkler service to flush the lines and the septic service when it backed up. He decorated the house, bought new fixtures, and rearranged the furniture. I gave my brief input, but it was mostly all his doing.

Then, suddenly, I was the sole owner of a twenty-acre property that needed care. I began to understand how much it took for Charlie to do all that he had done. I had not fully appreciated his contribution. I read a book called *The Five Love Languages* and learned that his language was service. I had not appreciated how much service he had provided without my asking. I have also learned that I can decorate the house and choose paint, floors, and fixtures. And if I can't or don't want to, I can hire people to do the work. I can change light bulbs, take the garbage to the dump, put out the recycling, and wash my sheets! While these changes appear to be practical lessons, it really was my soul's voice saying to me, "You can do this. You are capable; you are enough."

I spent a lot of time telling the story of Charlie's betrayal. People on planes, at social events, and elsewhere would ask why I had moved to Montana. That question opened the door to recite the sordid details of my husband's affair. In addition to telling the story, I saw Charlie and Norine on a somewhat regular basis since we had many of the same friends and were involved in the same spiritual work. In fact, for my own "self-development," our spiritual teacher had me sit near them at many social gatherings, meetings, and holiday parties. This situation continued for the eighteen months they lived in Whitefish.

Why did I subject myself to such torture? Why didn't I leave the area? I think I "drank the Kool-Aid." I was told it was for my own growth, and I believed those voices. Whether or not that was true, seeing them did force me to confront the huge and dramatic changes in my life. I could not ignore Charlie and Norine, sweep their affair under a rug, or pretend nothing had happened because Charlie and Norine were in my face on a regular basis for those eighteen months.

I thought the story of Charlie's betrayal would get old or I would stop telling it, but I must admit, it took years for me to do that. I was stuck in the story, hurting myself over and over again. Neither Charlie nor Norine cared about that; they didn't know I was stuck there, and probably didn't care.

But then, slowly, I recognized what I was doing to myself. I was focusing on them and how terrible they were when I needed to focus inward on myself. At first, my goal was simple: get through the day without thinking of Charlie the first thing in the morning and the last thing at night. Then it was to think of myself and be grateful rather than focus on the loss. Learning to smile again and even laugh took many months. Easy as it sounds, this internal work—rather than lashing out—took all my energy.

Turning inward also meant standing in my own boots and learning to hold my own boundaries. Should I ever become involved with someone again, I now realize that it should be "all about me." I need to manage my own insecurities, look inward when I want to point outward and make him wrong, and understand my projections. After many years, I began to feel that the betrayal and all that resulted from the betrayal occurred for my own development. Likewise, I have had to own my own choices and understand that this is *my* life—not anyone else's—whether that someone else is a spiritual teacher, friend, or ex-husband.

Part of living my life includes finding my own voice and making my own decisions. In arguments, Charlie often said he had to defend himself and used his logic and voice to "win." At other times, I did the same thing. But it felt like I routinely gave in when we argued. Similarly, I found myself physically walking behind him, instead of beside him. It was not a conscious choice, but it was a metaphor for how I behaved in relationships.

Eight years ago, my marriage fell apart, and so did I. I've spent many of those years since wandering around in my own desert. However, through this trauma and drama, I grew up emotionally and finally found myself mentally and physically, and started to make my own choices. Even more importantly, on a spiritual level, I have come home to myself, my true self. I couldn't have done it without Charlie and Norine. One day, I might even thank them for being the catalyst for me turning my life around, but that probably won't happen today.

· *Peggy A. Nagae* ·

I am grateful for these past eight years and all the ups and downs I have experienced. As the song goes, "I once was lost, but now I'm found." I found myself and I am grateful.

BODHISATTVA IN TRAINING
By Faren Bachelis

I LOVE HUMANITY. IT'S PEOPLE WHO ANNOY ME.

The thought struck me as I watched a Tibetan Buddhist master teach on compassion. He described human beings as flowers in a colorful garden.

"Buddhas are the master gardeners," Dzigar Kongtrul Rinpoche told his rapt Seattle audience. "Bodhisattvas are gardeners in training. We need to tend all the flowers equally with love and compassion."

I'd studied Buddhism long enough to understand that a Buddha is an enlightened being, and a bodhisattva is someone who aspires to enlightenment in order to benefit others. The bodhisattva path is open to anyone—even me. I worry about this, because to paraphrase Groucho Marx, I'm not sure I want to be a member of a club that would have me as a member.

I don't think I'm bodhisattva material. As much as I aspire to be an awakened being radiating love and compassion, I'm more comfortable radiating judgment and impatience. While I enjoy flowers as much as the next guy, I love some more than others, I find some noxious, and I'd like to take a weed whacker to a few.

Sure, I'd like to think I have the potential to become enlightened, to have an awakened heart. Buddha said everyone carries the seed of awakening within him or her, what he called basic goodness. But if he heard me let loose a string of expletives after some jerk has just cut me off on the freeway, the Buddha would probably point at me and say, "Well, everyone but *her*."

Maybe I'm just too, well, *human*. I can be petty, judgmental, controlling—imperfect. I see these behaviors in myself, but I just can't seem to get rid of them. The other morning a lone woman ahead of me at the drive-through espresso stand ordered *four* drinks, a breakfast sandwich (it took extra time to heat it), and a dog biscuit (presumably for her dog). I waited nearly eight minutes and would've left (I had a doctor's appointment), but I was hemmed in by the car behind me. When she finally drove off I threw her a nasty look in her rearview and then made a snide comment to the poor barista. *Oh, God,* I thought later. *I'm a horrible person! Why can't I be more patient?*

At his talk, Dzigar Kongtrul had said that it's all about our attitude. He'd reminded us that we already have perfect enlightenment as our essence. So if we believe that we are good just as we are, then we can develop even more goodness. If we believe that we are patient, then we can improve our patience, and so on. Zen teacher Shunryu Suzuki put it this way: "You're perfect just as you are. And you could use a little improvement."

It's the improvement part that trips me up. I often forget that when I ask for more patience, for example, I don't just magically become more patient. What usually happens is that I get a whole bunch of opportunities to *practice* patience. I'll encounter *more* slowpokes in the espresso line. Or in the grocery checkout line. Or in the fast lane on the freeway.

Buddhism appeals to me partly because it's a science of mind—it helps me understand how the mind works. You could say the Buddha was the first psychologist. And amazingly, although his teachings originated 2,500 years ago, they remain as fresh and relevant as they were when he attained his enlightenment under the Bodhi tree. He taught that "we are what we think. With our thoughts we make the world." Another way of putting it is that everything we experience outside of us is simply a projection of what's going on inside. So if I see angry people or sad people or fearful people, they're all a reflection of the angry, sad, fearful parts of me.

I read somewhere that if we make a list of people we don't like, we'll learn a lot about those aspects of ourselves that we can't face. Furthermore, those who repel us unwittingly show the aspects of ourselves that we find unacceptable. Being around people we dislike is often a catalyst for making friends with ourselves.

· We Came Back to Say ·

When I saw that, I thought, "Are you kidding? You mean to say I have an inner Rush Limbaugh? A Charles Manson? A Sarah Palin?" *Ewwwww!*

As unsettling as this realization is, I'm actually starting to get it. Decades of introspection, therapy, and spiritual practice have borne this out. As they say in twelve-step groups, it's an inside job. If I'm going to find any measure of self-acceptance, I'd better start from the inside out, not the other way around. One of the key points is the idea of embracing those parts of ourselves that we have rejected. "Hug your demons or they'll bite you in the ass," writes Pia Mellody.

Yeah, but if I'm going to dive in and start hugging my inner Rush, Charlie, and Sarah, I'll need a big dose of kindness and compassion for myself. And maybe a dose or two of Cuervo. As my Sufi friend Jamal says, this inner work is simple, but not easy. It's messy, scary, and frustrating. Enlightenment is definitely not for sissies.

Buddhists emphasize the importance of compassion, both for ourselves and for others. We need it for lots of reasons, not the least of which is to help us shine a light in the darkest recesses of our hearts. And when it comes to compassion, for Tibetan Buddhists the big kahuna is Chenrezig, the bodhisattva of compassion (called Avalokiteshvara in Sanskrit, Kwan-yin in Chinese). His Holiness the Dalai Lama is viewed as a living manifestation of Chenrezig, so this is a big deal.

Not that I'm an expert on Chenrezig. I'd never heard of him until a Buddhist friend recently suggested I attend an empowerment, which is a ritual that establishes a special connection between the participant and a Buddhist deity. A revered lama (a Tibetan spiritual teacher) had traveled to the States from India, and this was a rare opportunity to receive this initiation. I'd read that meditation on Chenrezig is especially effective for those who want to be compassionate and kind to all beings—including ourselves.

I didn't know what I was in for on that July afternoon, but I hoped to find my inner Buddha. I was ready for transformation. Ready to release decades of self-aversion, confusion, fear, and judgment of both myself and others. I really wanted to replace all that with understanding, compassion, and acceptance. I just wanted to be happy.

I'd found the temple easily enough. The buttercup-yellow, two-story clapboard building was festooned with fluttering Tibetan prayer flags.

It looked as if it'd been uprooted from Dharamsala and plopped right in the middle of Seattle's Greenwood neighborhood.

I sat at the back of the large shrine room, which felt cluttered—nearly every square foot was covered with colorful tapestries, bright banners hanging from the ceiling, vivid iconic art depicting tantric deities. Aside from the monks—who were actual Tibetans—most of the aspirants were white, middle-class, and middle-aged Seattleites who dressed like they'd been practicing meditation and eating gluten-free for years: hemp yoga pants, pashmina shawls draped carefully around toned shoulders, natural fiber shirts and drawstring pants and flowing skirts. Everyone looked so relaxed, so organic, so—Buddhist.

At the front, the carmine-robed lama rested serenely upon crossed legs, eyes closed, a trimmed peacock feather in one hand. Joined by three other monks, he chanted a blessing for those seated before him.

"May you attain Buddhahood to benefit all sentient beings," said the Venerable Geshe Kunchok Tenzin.

Since this was my first experience with a Tibetan Buddhist initiation, I had mixed expectations and limited understanding of what it involved. But I knew that something profound and powerful was happening. I felt it in the room, in the monks' sonorous chanting, in the bright afternoon light bouncing off dust motes jitterbugging throughout the room like millions of tiny Shivas ...

An hour into the ceremony and I was miserable. I knew I should've sat in a chair instead of on this flimsy cushion at the Buddhist temple. My arthritic knees were aching, but I'd wanted to fit in. I tried to pay attention as clouds of cloyingly sweet incense burned my eyes and nose. I'd skipped lunch and was obsessing about the Snickers bar in my purse that I'd planned to have after my imminent spiritual awakening. The people around me all looked so peaceful. I was certain none of them were fantasizing about chocolate and dinner. A young mother pulled out an ivory breast and started nursing. I tried not to stare. I stared anyhow.

By now I was pretty sure I wasn't cut out for enlightenment.

The American translator told us that the lama would impart special blessings to us. A young monk handed the holy man with burnished skin and a beatific smile a small candle holder with several lit candles. *Okay, focus,* I admonished myself, and took a mindful breath. A deep peace settled through the room and, slowly, over me ...

Thump. Thump. Thump.

A loud pounding pulled me out of my tranquil state. I looked around to see where the noise was coming from.

Thump-thump-thump-thump-thump.

A curly haired toddler hopped down the creaky wooden stairs at the back of the room, then loudly clomped up the aisle toward the monks. His thirtyish mom sat calmly, oblivious to Junior's marching back and forth. Maybe she'd already reached nirvana. Maybe she was on Zoloft.

Clomp. Clomp. Clomp.

The little boy had hopped down the aisle back to the stairs. He was hanging off the handrail, legs dangling between the posts, stubby-toed bare feet slapping on a step. Right next to my head.

Okay, I thought. *This is a good thing. Here's an opportunity to practice patience and nonjudgment. I can accept the whole shebang: monks, meditators, traffic, and this annoying kid.*

The lama continued his prayers, slowly waving the peacock feather. He seemed unfazed by the activity. Well, yeah, he's spiritually evolved. Me, I've been so distracted by Junior's antics I didn't hear a word of what the translator just said. For all I know, he could've told us we've all just erased a thousand lifetimes of bad karma from our past lives. Or a year's worth of parking tickets. Or maybe he asked one of the monks to get the rice on the stove, because we'd be done soon.

That made me start thinking about dinner, until I sensed I was being stared at. A pair of bright button eyes had me fixed in their inquisitive gaze. From his perch on the banister, just inches from me, the kid studied me intently. I did the same, momentarily tempted to stick my tongue out at him. I didn't—it'd be spiritually incorrect.

Junior lost interest in this interaction and focused his attention on the front of the room again. Then: *thump thump thump,* he ran up the aisle, throwing his arms around a man seated on a cushion smack in front of the lama. The man—his father?—remained still. The boy danced around the man. I watched the man, the boy, and the lama. Nobody seemed to be at all distracted or annoyed by this.

Except me.

Jeez, what's wrong with these parents? I wondered. *How clueless are they to not understand that children this young shouldn't be brought to*

this kind of event if they can't sit for long periods. How thoughtless of them. How insensitive. How stupid and rude—
Then, abruptly, *Oh for chrissake, what's wrong with* me?

This led to my rapid descent into the dreaded and all-too-familiar black hole of self-criticism, self-doubt, and unworthiness, and the conviction that I was doomed to remain stuck in the cycle of suffering because I'd accrued too much bad karma. Translated as: You don't deserve happiness, it's hopeless, so you might as well accept it and give up the search for enlightenment. And go get a cheeseburger and large fries instead.

I scanned the room, imagining that everyone else was so much more spiritually advanced than me. They *looked* more spiritual, they sat so easily on their cushions. Some even had performed the formal full prostrations at the beginning of the empowerment. They surely must be closer to the bodhisattva ideal than I'd ever be.

I was considering leaving when the lama seemed to look right at me and said, "Receiving an initiation is like planting a seed. Properly cultivated with the right conditions, this seed will sprout and help you grow into the enlightened state of Buddhahood."

As I sat there thinking about seeds and gardens and Buddhahood, I remembered Dzigar Kongtrul Rinpoche's metaphor of humanity as a colorful garden. "When you walk into a garden you see this flower, that flower, this plant, that plant," he'd said. "All come from a seed, and though all are different, they are all one in the garden. Just as you can enjoy the variety of the flowers, you can appreciate human beings as well."

Maybe it was the late afternoon light, the incense clouding my eyes. Maybe it was just low blood sugar. But when I momentarily closed my eyes I was no longer seated uncomfortably in a Tibetan Buddhist shrine room. I was standing in the middle of a beautiful garden filled with roses and lilacs, snapdragons, poppies, jonquils—and thousands of other flowers. The lama was a yellow lotus, the little boy a pink rosebud, his mother a hyacinth, the translator a daisy. And I saw myself, watering can in hand, tending lovingly to all of them. And in the center of the garden was a single red rose—and I realized that rose was me.

The image faded as quickly as it had appeared and I was back in the shrine room—in my body, with the monks and the seekers. Maybe I was beginning to understand what they both had to teach me—the holy man and the curly haired boy. I pulled the Snickers bar from my purse and decided to stay a little longer.

THE UPSIDE OF LOSS
By Star Roberts

THE BATHROOM FAUCET WE'VE LEFT ON for our fifteen-year-old cat (who refuses to drink from her dish) drips, and the sound I hear is loss, loss, loss. It is 3:43 a.m. and my post-menopausal brain is riding a roller coaster of thoughts, keeping me awake at a time when my body needs sleep, craves sleep, and yet somehow avoids sleep. Often, at night when my mind just won't shut off, it pulls out the mental file cabinet marked "Writing" and riffles through to make sense of my story. Now I'm ruminating on a theme for my memoir, or rather, threading my way through the theme that has picked me. My bedside clock ticks, loss, loss, loss.

The first loss I remember happened in 1960 when I was five, a few days after Christmas in our tiny Oregon logging town. It was a cold, late afternoon and steely fog fingered the hillside outside our little green house. Inside, excitement ramped up. We were going to Grandma's to exchange Christmas presents, and chaos bounced off the wood-paneled walls.

"You can each bring one toy with you," Mom said, as five kids commenced bumping into each other like pinballs, scooping up toys to show Grandma.

Chipper, our pet chipmunk, was in his cage by the living room window. He got caught up in the energy of the room and started scattering his shredded newspaper. My brother George had captured him at Crater Lake the summer before. Despite that, Chipper was a smart cookie. He'd stand there with his fingers wrapped around the bars of his cage, looking like a furry convict planning his escape from the Big House. And when no one was looking, he'd reach his tiny hands through the door and flip the latch. Frequently, he was our early morning alarm clock, running through the bedrooms, skittering across our faces, wake up, wake up!

But he couldn't go to Grandma's, so I'd picked my Basket-O-Kittens to take with me. They weren't real kittens—Dad was allergic—so I'd asked Santa for the white, fluffy Persians I'd seen in the Sears catalogue. The mama cat's eyes were marbled blue glass, and the three babies were her exactly, but miniature, with matching blue ribbons. They nested together in a wicker basket, the kittens somehow attached to the mama, the Mama to the basket, so you couldn't take just one. They couldn't be separated.

"You can't bring them, Honey, we don't have room in the car," Mom said as I tried to get out the door with my Basket-O-Kittens. "You'll have to pick something smaller."

That's how I got stuck with the hard, plastic baby doll that didn't pee or do anything.

The details of how we learned our house was on fire are lost for me in the ether. My next clear memory kicks in later that evening, when we're all accounted for (my oldest brother, Dana, had been at a scout meeting; Dad at a bar) and reunited at the High Lakes Café—a place I'd pined for longingly but never been in before that night. It sat across the highway from where our house used to be, and where the fire truck lights now flash in my memory, blinking loss, loss, loss.

But this is the image that hangs vivid in my mind: We're sitting around a yellow, Formica table in the middle of the cafe dining room and a waitress with crinkly eyes and an impressive beehive comes over and says, "Just order anything you want, this one's on us." It's my first time eating in a sit-down restaurant and I'm thrilled. My decision is made easy by the pictures on the menu: The Broasted Chicken Basket.

When our order comes, all my senses laser-beam on the hot, juicy chicken and crinkly fries, all golden and floating on a white paper cloud in a red plastic basket. I feel bliss as it's placed in front of me. Then, I look out the window and see what's left of our house, glowing in the distance, and it occurs to me maybe I shouldn't be so happy. But it didn't kick in until much later that Chipper and my Basket-O-Kittens were gone for good.

As a kid, I didn't understand the permanence of loss. In fact, that chicken basket was a definite upside in my mind. For a long time, I didn't know our losses connect to one another. I thought they were each their own separate event. Now, as a woman flirting with the final third of her life, I know better. With each new loss, I feel the emotional thread that connects it back to the ones before.

Losses that started popping onto one another in the early snap-beads of my childhood have gained greater worth with time. They've shown me what's important and morphed from plastic into pearls, each one sliding onto a string of memories, threading back through a lifetime.

This is how I can now see the upside in my almost comically disastrous childhood. After that first house fire, we lost everything again in the Christmas flood of '64 and then, unbelievably, a couple of years later our next house burned to the ground shortly after my twelfth birthday.

I remember a conversation with my mom as we were packing up our temporary rental a few weeks after the second fire. My parents had decided to move from Oregon to Washington, hoping to change our string of bad luck. While we loaded up Dad's camper truck and our old Chevy station wagon with our few possessions, thunder rumbled in the distance. God was bowling. I could see a summer storm making its way down the Umpqua Valley, and my nostrils filled with the smell of wet dirt as the first fat raindrops plopped in the dust.

"Mom," I said, throwing pillows into the car, "can you tell me what we did to piss God off?" Admittedly, my faith was rattled by then. It was hard not to take two fires and a flood personally.

The thing to know about my mom is that she could find the upside in just about anything (though today a trained professional might call it denial), but her response stuck with me.

"I don't think he's pissed off, Honey, I think he just knows we can handle more than most people." Hearing it that way made me feel like she'd given me my own secret super power to draw on when I needed it. And still, today, I'm pretty sure it's true.

I wonder if losses (and super powers) aren't passed on from one generation to the next, like hair color or height. I ponder this when I think of my daughter Riley's first real loss, her friend Rachel, who was six when she died in a plane crash. Up until then, Riley had been living a life with few worries or cares and never experienced loss beyond a goldfish or two. She was a happy, well-adjusted kiddo living a pretty cushy childhood on Queen Anne Hill, a girl who didn't yet need super powers.

On the morning after the plane crash, she and I walked to John Hay Elementary School like we did every weekday. We didn't know yet that day was different. Soon enough though, I felt a palpable darkness in the air that couldn't be attributed solely to Seattle in January. I took note and grabbed Riley's hand when it followed us into the building. It crept into my consciousness in the downward glances and the hushed voices in the hallway, whispering loss, loss, loss.

In Riley's kindergarten classroom—across the hall from the classroom Rachel wouldn't be coming back to—the curtains were drawn, and the room was dim. Miss Wick directed kids to sit on the rug (crisscross-applesauce) while she asked parents to stop by the office on their way out.

There I learned Alaska flight 261 had gone down the night before. Two John Hay families had been on board, and there were no survivors.

I remember Rachel as a bright light. Her dimples and golden curls lit up the room in a millennium Shirley Temple kind of way. She and Riley had known each other since preschool and because she was a grade ahead, Rachel had taken Riley under her wing. On their way out to recess she always gave Riley a giant bear hug and watched out for her on the playground, showing her the ropes. Only two months earlier Rachel had laughed with gapped-tooth glee, posing for a picture at Riley's birthday party.

When I picked Riley up from school that day, I struggled to make sense of it for her, to find the words to explain the unexplainable. My super powers were missing in action. In the end, we bought two little stuffed bears, each hugging a heart that read "I Love You" and took one of them over to Rachel's house and gave it to her grandparents. Riley said that way she and Rachel would each have one to remember the other.

In the middle of grief, especially when children are involved, it's hard to see the upside of loss, to remember that it's balanced out on the other side with joy, and that one cannot exist without the other.

There is a Buddhist saying that the most beautiful lotus grows through the deepest mud. I hold onto this thought when I'm in the thick of it.

The sediment of losses in my life, and now my daughter's, started accumulating early on. Only now, with time and distance, and looking through the silty lens of past experience, I can see that loss is a gift, even if it's one I wouldn't want to give anyone. It's a reminder that some things are replaceable—houses, possessions, clothes—and some things are not—beloved pets, family, friends. The upside of loss is being reminded to appreciate the irreplaceable.

Motherhood and plane crashes took up a lot of my thoughts at the end of January 2000. In fact, it would take the next irreplaceable person in my life to get me on a plane again, only three short weeks later: my son, Zyan Van Than, newly born and waiting in a Cambodian orphanage half a world away.

The night before we left for Cambodia, my best friend Linda came over to say goodbye and bring a present for Riley. We'd become friends in middle school, thirty years earlier. She won me over in eighth grade English class, spring quarter, when she casually sauntered over to the window, opened it up and let one rip like it was the most natural thing in the world. And that summer when she morphed from horn-rim-wearing geek to contact-lens-wearing babe (and I continued my late-blooming slump) she still included me in her orbit, clinching our friendship in perpetuity.

What really connected us though, were our losses. We knew quite literally where each other's bodies were buried. She knew mine: brother in a hunting accident; father by suicide. And I knew hers: high school boyfriend in a freak pole-vaulting accident; father, slowly, with brain cancer. Through the years we'd shared losses and joys, and she'd remained my wisecracking, sharp-minded, best friend with just enough mush and raunch thrown in for me to overlook when she went into a funk and dropped out of sight for months at a time.

But that night she was present and thoughtful. She knew our focus would be on Zyan when we got back from Cambodia, and she wanted Riley to know that her promotion from Only Child to Big Sister was a Big Deal.

"Here you go, Missy, something just for you," she said, handing over a little bag Riley quickly tore into, coming up with a powder blue T-shirt punctuated with daisies.

"Thanks LindaCarter!" Riley squealed, running her first and last names together like the super hero she thought she was.

Then Linda handed me some supplies for the orphanage and said, "Well, I guess I'll mosey so you can finish packing." She headed out the door and lingered on the porch, so I followed her out. I could tell she wanted to say something else, maybe without little ears listening. She leaned against the railing, looking down into the yard, and it was then I noticed she was a little shaky.

"I wanted you to know if you don't hear from me when you get back it's because I'm going into rehab."

"Oh, Honey, I'm so glad you're doing this. I've been worried."

"I know, I know," she said, and we shared a long, full-frontal hug (her specialty). "I'm sure I'll be whipped into shape in no time."

I'd spent the better part of a year buried in home studies, background checks, and reams of paperwork preparing for our son's adoption. I hadn't said anything about the overpowering smell of mouthwash on her breath when we walked Green Lake. Or how she'd just moved her soup around in her bowl the last time we went to lunch. I hadn't prepared for Linda going into rehab and not coming out.

When we got back home from Cambodia a week later, Linda's husband called to say she'd taken a down turn and been moved out of rehab and into the hospital. I took Zyan to see her the next day so she could admire him up close, thinking it might cheer her up. She'd oohed and aahed but her eyes were yellow and her stomach bloated. Still, I thought it was just a matter of time before she'd be better.

I had a tiny new baby, and I was preoccupied when she died in the hospital a few weeks later. I saw her awake only once more before, unbelievably, she slipped into a coma, then away.

Not ready to deal with her death, its black pearl of grief slipped onto my loss necklace unmourned. Six years later, when my mother died, Linda's death came rushing back to me, reminding me that if we forget to grieve, our bodies store up losses like nuts put away for our winters of sadness. They wait for us to bring them out and crack open their stories.

It seems when new loss comes, it brings old grief forward to be reexamined once again. And when I can't sleep, it's a thirsty old cat, dripping loss, loss, loss in my ear, reminding me to live with it, write through it, own it, because grief never leaves. It only moves around to surprise me in a new location.

When that happens (or sometimes much later), I try to remember the upside of loss; it also informs and expands our capacity for joy. Loss helps us appreciate the irreplaceable. The next time grief slides a pearl onto my necklace of life's losses, depending on my mood or the strength of my super powers at that moment, I'll either saunter over to the window and let one rip or put a lotus in my hair and remember that it is through the mud we reach beauty.

A PERSON OF COLOR

By Sandy Barnes

What a surprise for me, as a middle-aged woman, to realize that I belonged to an ethnic group other than 'white.'

One busy morning in the mid-1990s, I joined a group of harried parents squeezed into a crowded classroom for an adult education program while our small children attended class at the progressive Jewish religious school. The rabbi at the adult class stated her challenge: she would give a history of the Jewish people in forty-five minutes. Lightning fast.

We all knew that the Jews started out in the Middle East. The Chosen People of Israel. The stories from the Torah. The Jews scattered from their ancestral lands to all parts of the world after the destruction of the Temple in Jerusalem. One group, the Sephardim, moved through the Mediterranean and Northern Africa. The dominant group, the Ashkenazim, settled in parts of Europe. The rabbi whipped through centuries of history, expulsions, pogroms, migrations. She made it all the way through before our children were done with their classes.

At the end, she paused and a parent asked, "So you're saying that all of us who thought we were European are of Middle Eastern descent?"

"The Jewish people ... that's where we started," answered the rabbi.

"My grandparents told me that their families came from Prussia and Odessa," he replied.

Another said, "My great-grandfather was born in a village in Poland."

Germany, others added. Austria. Bavaria. Ukraine.

The majority of Jews in America have Ashkenazi ancestors descended from the Jews from Central and Eastern Europe. Including me.

I grew up in the California suburbs full of white people, in the 1950s and 1960s. Neither my elementary nor my high school included very many Asian or Hispanic kids. My parents unwittingly taught us to treat the only black student, Julie, a well-mannered daughter of a physician, with condescension. They modeled overly solicitous behavior and insincere inclusion, always making sure we included Julie whether she wanted to come or not.

My parents both left their native New England cities full of extended family and heartily embraced assimilation with other educated, post-war families, eager to leave any ethnic roots behind. They joined the West Coast migration where opportunities abounded for everybody in the California sunshine.

"Being Jewish is just another religion," my mother had told me when I was in elementary school. "It just means that your family goes to a different place to worship. We belong to the temple, but it's just like a different church. You don't look any different. Nobody will know you're Jewish if you don't tell them," she assured me. "And it doesn't matter anyway. You are the same as everybody else."

I believed my mother. Just the same as the other kids who lived in the California suburbs with their winding streets with Spanish names. The single-story homes that lined the streets all had big front lawns dotted with chugging sprinklers. The families I knew included a working dad and a stay-at-home mom. White, from European descendants. As children, several generations removed from emigration, we compared the European countries of our ancestry: Scotland, France, Germany, Sweden. Me too. "My ancestors came mostly from Germany," I said.

Now, as an adult sitting in the room with all of the other Jewish parents, it hit me: did I have true European ancestry? Did I really share common European roots with the other kids I grew up with?

My Ashkenazi ancestors, these European Jews descended from the Middle Eastern Semitic populations in the distant, hazy past, did not always live peaceably with the Slavic, Latin, and Germanic peoples whose countries they inhabited. Pogroms—deadly riots accompanied by rape and murder—and expulsions marred their history in Europe.

Another parent suggested the very idea on my mind: "So maybe these Jewish immigrants weren't *really* European?"

Maybe I had a different German heritage than my neighbors, I thought.

More specifically, those neighbors in my childhood were white, and I was not.

I tossed this idea around in my mind.

Another parent posed a question. "Look at us, do we look white?"

I warily looked around the room at the other parents, sneaking a peek and wondering, for the first time, what 'looking white' meant. At the same time, I thought of my own dark features shared across my family members. Around the room, I saw dark curly hair, olive skin, some prominent facial features and lots of brown eyes with a certain soft look about them. And these adults definitely had a thing or two to say.

We didn't look white. Or sound white. Or act white. I hadn't thought of myself quite like this before—as part of an ethnic group.

That's not what my mother would have said. "Our family has lived in New Haven for generations," she told me. "Your great-grandfather Morris Baumann owned the Baumann Rubber Company that employed over two hundred people. Your great-great-grandfather Maier Zunder served on the school board; he had a school named after him. And another of your great-grandfathers, Charles Weil, was a police commissioner."

She proudly showed me the gold watch owned by my police commissioner great-grandfather and the pictures of Zunder School.

Definitely mainstream establishment. We didn't come from those *shtetls*, those small towns in central and eastern Europe with largely observant orthodox Jewish populations dramatized in "Fiddler on the Roof." None of that foreign-born Yiddish business in my family. The affluent High German Jews of my mother's family had been in America for over a century; they looked down on the later emigrants. We were as European as our neighbors. Same as everybody else.

As a child, I could never understand how adults in my community knew I was Jewish. The name Ginsburgh? German, European like all the other kids, right? And lots of other kids had dark hair and eyes. How did those people know I was Jewish? And I felt a little uncomfortable when they did know. Like I should feel ashamed or hide that I was Jewish.

My parents generally stayed silent about our family being different from the rest of the community. They didn't consider it important to live in an area with more Jewish families in the neighborhood. But my mother went straight to the principal when a seventh-grade teacher singled me out as she explained that most Jews had big noses.

I looked back at my senior picture in the high school yearbook and the young, dark-eyed girl with the wavy, dark hair stared back at me. I definitely did not look like everybody else on that yearbook page. It seemed so obvious that there was some ethnic thing going on despite my parents' denials.

I realized the truth. I looked Jewish and had a Jewish name. Why should I be so surprised? I occupied a minority niche in my own society. Nobody in the majority can understand how that feels. The slights and value judgments had grated on me. The winter holiday condescension. The portrayal of Jews as primitive old men mumbling in some ancient language who didn't even have the New Testament, just that old one. The aggrieved concerned looks of the true believers, worried that you could never go to Heaven.

I admit, as a child, I also worried about going to Heaven. Some of the girls in the fourth grade were talking about it.

"I heard at church that if I say the Lord's Prayer and love Jesus, then I will go to heaven when I die," said April one day on the playground.

"I know, if you accept Jesus into your heart, then you have nothing to worry about. You get to live forever. We'll all meet Jesus! Way up high!" agreed Barbara.

I listened hard. I had never heard about this before.

"But not everybody gets to go to heaven. Only those who believe in Jesus and go to church," replied April grimly. "The rest," she paused, "well, the rest have to go to Hell," she added with a shiver.

"It sounds awful, down there with the Devil, burning up. In my church, they told me if I love Jesus right now, then I won't go to Hell," said Barbara. "I love Jesus," she added, looking sidewise at me.

"Me too," answered April. "I love Jesus, too."

They both turned to look at me.

"What about you, Sandy, do you love Jesus?" April asked.

I mumbled something. I didn't know what to say.

"What church do you go to?" asked Barbara.

"My church is the Jewish temple across town," I said softly.

They both looked shocked and quickly walked off. "You know, the Jews killed Jesus," Barbara called over her shoulder.

I stood there crestfallen and ashamed. Did the Jews really kill Jesus? This God of my neighbors excluded me and my family from Heaven. Forever. I read the Jesus Christ section in our *World Book Encyclopedia* over and over trying to make sense of it. My family didn't want to talk about it. I sensed that they considered this a forbidden subject.

My siblings and all of my cousins have participated in a huge demographic shift: we all married non-Jews. Didn't that follow from an assimilationist stand? My husband and I made a conscious choice to raise our children in a Jewish family. Looking back, I realized I experienced latent anti-Semitism from my in-laws. They loved and accepted me and supported our marriage, but I think they viewed my being Jewish as rather a shame. I really didn't have to bring up that Jewish stuff, did I? The quaint Hanukah imagery could never measure up to the marvelous American Christmas. My husband's parents would sneak in baby Jesus books that my husband and I would throw away. "Won't you please let the kids have just a little Christmas tree?" my mother-in-law pleaded. "We could put it downstairs and you wouldn't even have to look at it." I ignored her. She couldn't understand that I considered her remarks disrespectful. I could choose the activities that I wished to emphasize in my own home. I did not take Christmas away from my children, look around, it's everywhere, even in our own household.

Recently a distant relative from my husband's side invited my husband and me for dinner at their home, for the first time, after knowing us almost 20 years. They had learned from my blog that I was Jewish, and they seemed quite concerned. They asked me about the dinner they prepared several times before I realized that they were worried that I wouldn't eat it; that I might reject their hospitality. I could see that they didn't know quite what to expect. The evening went very well. I wondered, was it possible that they had never met a Jewish person before?

Even more recently, my husband and I hosted a Thanksgiving dinner for his extended (not Jewish) family. Besides our adult children, my husband's two brothers and their families along with some aunts and uncles chatted in our living room lined with pictures of my prominent New Haven Jewish ancestors. My mother's pride, her 'Delia wall'—a group of photographs and items belonging to her grandmother, Delia, daughter of Maier Zunder—hung over my fireplace. A beautiful lace fan framed on rich, dark velvet with a golden painted wood frame took center stage.

My niece Katherine had invited her new boyfriend, Mark, a tall, slim young man with a ready smile. I liked his gracious manner, how comfortable he acted with the grandmothers and aunts and uncles.

"What are you up to, Mark?" I asked. I'm the aunt; I get to ask things like this.

"I'm a youth minister at a church in North Bend," he replied proudly, "and I'm studying for the ministry."

"Oh, so you're taking classes?" He nodded. "What are you taking this term?" I asked.

"Right now, Biblical Hebrew," he told me.

"Oh, are you learning to read Hebrew?" I asked. I knew that he and Katherine participated in an evangelical Christian ministry.

"Some," he said with a smile.

"Have you gone to any Jewish services or a synagogue, to use it? To see how it works?"

"Um, well no, but maybe sometime I should do that, I guess."

"I'll be glad to go with you, if you want, to go to Friday night Shabbat services. Temple Beth Am is nearby," I suggested, referring to a nearby Reform congregation. "Dennis, too," I added, looking at my husband.

"Sure, be glad to. We just went to Yom Kippur services a few weeks ago. Where was it?" Dennis said.

"At Kol Haneshemah, a progressive congregation that's based in West Seattle," I replied.

"I liked it, lots of people there," my husband said. "Good music."

"They did a great job with the Kol Nidre. I always love that, I can't miss it."

Mark squirmed a bit. Nobody else said anything.

"The Kol Nidre is an ancient prayer only said at the Yom Kippur evening service," I offered. "The most important moment of the year. Very solemn and quiet."

I turned to Mark. "I don't know if they are including that sort of thing in your class."

"Um, I don't know," said the young man, "I don't think so."

He seemed a little wary. Maybe worried that some old men with funny clothes will chant an ancient primitive prayer and he won't know what to do? Maybe he feels he would betray his faith just by walking in the door? I would think that he would want to learn about Judaism since he was taking Hebrew.

I was pleased that my husband had brought up the Erev Yom Kippur service as it gave us the opportunity to talk about Jewish events as normal. Because, for us, Jewish life is normal.

Since that day at the religious school, I've identified myself as a person of color. As a member of the outside world where everything looks different, I no longer have to pretend to be like everybody else. I've admitted to myself that I don't belong to the privileged majority class, no matter what I thought before. The way will never be as clear for me. I know that I will continue to expect some condescension, whispered comments, and tacit exclusion.

The nagging worry of being found out has disappeared because I am no longer hiding anything. My feeling that others might sometimes exclude me begins to make sense.

I am neither white nor Christian.

I don't completely reject my parents' assimilationist aspirations. They saw themselves as pioneers staking their claim in California, where almost everybody came from somewhere else. They fervently believed that their family could completely join the white mainstream and, most of the time, the strategy worked. But not always and not completely.

THE MOTH OF MIRTH
By Julie Parks

YOU COULD ALL BE DEAD. My variation on advice for suppressing the fear of public speaking: imagine the audience completely naked. I looked at the unfamiliar people in the funeral home. I only recognized my few family members. The others were teaching colleagues or his bug and weed friends. *You could be dead too*, I thought as their strange faces turned toward the lectern.

My family is ruled by the Sign of Cancer. A kaleidoscope of melanoma, breast cancer, lymphomas. Cousin Paul succumbed to multiple myeloma. A cancer of the blood. An accumulation of hyperactive, mis-dividing plasma cells. And I had decided to speak at his memorial service.

Cousin Paul was not a real cousin. A cousin-in-law. A relative relative. Canadian. He was married to my first cousin Margot. After Margot died, my husband and I stayed in touch with Paul and his daughter—my first cousin once removed. Although it always seemed that it was Margot who was the first cousin once removed. By cancer.

Cousin Paul was odd, unique, quirky. He liked to bird watch and would take daytrips with his family to explore the woods, fields, and marshes around Toronto. But he would leave his mother and young daughter in the car while he wandered off by himself. One afternoon after being left for several hours, his daughter heard a rustling noise in the bushes. Excitedly she ran to greet her father. "Oh no," she cried to her grandmother, "it's a sheep!"

· *We Came Back to Say* ·

Whenever we think of Paul, my husband and I think of moths. Once Paul almost hurled himself through a plate-glass restaurant window in his enthusiasm for identifying the genus, the species, the phylum, the whatever of the attached insects. Moths. Attracted by dinner candlelight. Moths, indistinguishable from one another as flecks of dandruff.

Some of Cousin Paul's extreme behavior might have been symptomatic of his disease. My family just considered him a bit peculiar like his mother, who, at ninety-four while on a senior outing to Las Vegas, broke her arm playing the slot machines. Or who, after her husband passed away, returned to the store the almost new mattress upon which he had died.

My husband could not attend Paul's funeral. But he can never forget a visit in 1999, four years previously. Cousin Paul and his girlfriend, Catherine, had stayed with us in Seattle on their way to a rock garden convention in Oregon. Paul was retired, traveled around the world, and took high blood pressure medicine because of his strenuous lifestyle of single-mindedly reclaiming Canada's native weeds and moths from the onslaught of alien species. American and English.

They arrived at our house on a Friday evening. Saturday morning Paul, Catherine, and I went to Kubota Gardens, which has an abundance of Pacific Northwest flora and fauna displayed in a Japanese manner. It took quite a while to drive there because Paul and Catherine had to catalogue every roadside plant. They loved the garden. Giant rain-foresty weeds, waterfalls, butterflies. Paul managed to identify the weeds rather than pull them out. In Toronto, on a walk in a park, Paul would yell, "LIVERWORT, ALIEN!" and yank the offending vegetation out of the ground. He never was arrested, but posthumously he received horticultural awards.

In the afternoon my husband joined us for a stroll in the Arboretum. Cousin Paul was armed with two cameras, a tripod, four books (butterflies, birds, weeds and flowers, trees), and a butterfly net. As he wielded the net, people would stare and ask us, "Is that a real butterfly net?" I would reply, "No. It's really a Canadian tennis racket."

After supper Paul set up his moth-collecting apparatus in our back yard. At the time we had a nervous neighbor. She would call the police over the slightest unusual sound or disturbance. I warned her about Cousin Paul's impending visit. "Don't be alarmed if one night next weekend you see someone in the yard flapping around in a white sheet. It won't be the Ku Klux Klan, just an eccentric relative (by marriage) trying to attract nocturnal bugs. Nothing to worry about … "

Paul draped the sheet over the fence. He brought out a mercury-vapor light and hung it from a ladder. The cord wasn't long enough to reach the electrical outlet. He got out his new, lightweight, travel extension cord. It didn't fit the plug. Paul poked and pushed and turned the prongs. The light went on and off. Finally the apparatus was entomologically correct. No moths. A flea showed up on the reflective sheet. A fruit fly. Paul was running in and out of the house.

"It's too cold," he cried, "it's too windy."

I spotted a moth. "Paul. Paul. A moth! A moth! My credibility for a moth!"

Cousin Paul was very contemptuous of this first sighting. It was a diminutive half-inch. Not worthy of his attention. And not a western moth either, but a common eastern variety found also in Toronto. Paul caught it in a jar anyway. After dessert we checked the activity again. Two larger moths were circling the light. Paul captured the two in his jars. Turned out they had come from England! Paul had his moth book out, but he was hard-pressed to identify the variety with 100 illustrated moths per page. The book was forty to fifty years old; the colors were the blurry, orange-brown of early printed color photographs. Paul was surprised when I found several moths in the house. "How did they get in?" he puzzled.

Over coffee, Catherine entertained us with appetizing descriptions of their trip to Costa Rica. "The cockroaches were huge and beautifully striped in red and yellow. We didn't have any in our room. We had lizards on the wall."

Catherine also recounted loving details of birthing chrysalises in her house. A colleague had twenty extra cigar-sized pupae which he shared with Catherine. (I regret not asking extra from what!) Catherine nurtured the pupae and watched the moths emerge from the cocoons and unfold their hand-size wings. Some of the chrysalises failed to open. Catherine induced labor with a pair of scissors. Tough cutting. Too late. The wings had dried up.

Cousin Paul and Catherine drove away on Sunday morning. They had left the information and itinerary for the conference back in Toronto; we pointed them in the direction of the Washington coast and Oregon.

"It was like being in a Monty Python movie!" my husband commented while waving goodbye.

"Yes," I replied, "and I'll bet those desiccated insects were perfect for dipping in chocolate."

Paul used to end his letters with a line or two from a poem. I wanted to conclude his memorial service with a relevant quote. Moths are not as inspirational to poets as are butterflies, but in a book of English verse I found a reference by Percy B. Shelley.

I looked around the funeral home at the expectant faces; I clutched the lectern. One more *You will all be dead someday* for courage (carefully excluding myself from such an eventuality). Then I spoke, briefly reminiscing, and in conclusion I read out loud Shelley's poem. The words capturing Paul's curious, restive spirit ...

" ... the desire of the moth for the star,

Of the night for the morrow,

The devotion to something afar

From the sphere of our sorrow."

Today, when my husband and I see a moth flickering out from the night shadows into lamplight, or a moth clings to our living-room window—wings folding, unfolding—we have to laugh. A visitation. A reincarnation. Irrepressible Paul!

EAT ME

By John Mace

Hin Loon wasn't anything special to look at, outside or in. It was one of the typical Mom-and-Pop Asian restaurants in Seattle's International District. The neighborhood wasn't called "Chinatown" as in other cities; the Chinese had never really taken a big foothold in Seattle. Instead, Japanese, Hmong, Vietnamese, Laotian, Cambodian, and a flavoring of Chinese congregated in the six-by-ten block area south of the touristy Pioneer Square district.

Originally, Pioneer Square housed Seattle's elite; the streets were named for famous or infamous city fathers. Now it housed the techno crowd, trendy tattoo/piercing boutiques, and Oriental rug stores that were constantly going out of business or moving down the street, pretending to be new and unique. My office was in the Pioneer Square Building, a lovingly preserved artifact of Seattle's booming timbertown days, its Romanesque revival façade typical of Victorian-era tastes. In modern times, the International District served as the dining spot for those tourists and residents, adventuresome souls, brave enough to sample foods more exotic than what was offered on McDonald's dollar menu.

Hin Loon was not decorated with dragons, red Chinese lamps, or even painted with any Feng Shui pattern. Florescent lights illuminated white linoleum floors scratched over the years by steel framed tables and black Naugahyde chairs patched with silver duct tape. The attraction of this famed hole-in-the-wall was its fish tank located next to the dinky, cashier podium. Two hundred gallons of green algae water and dinner swam through bubbles blown in by motorized life

· *We Came Back to Say* ·

support. Dozens of fish the size of dinner plates groped their way through the light-green muck they ate before becoming dinner for the culinary explorers.

My wingman, Leon, had been assigned by a swank, techno foodie magazine to review the main attraction at Hin Loon. After finding parking on the narrow brick streets, I spied Leon standing outside with his boyfriend looking apprehensive about walking in as a couple. It was an amazing paradox: Leon grew up outside of Salt Lake City in a good Mormon family, attending Stake meetings, baptisms in Temple and Sunday dinners with family eating pot roast. Mormons are not known for their culinary explorations.

Eventually, in the call to be authentic and one week before his eternal marriage to a good Mormon girl, he escaped to Seattle. Leon dove headfirst into the debauchery found in dimly lit backrooms, 25 cent movies, groans and moans only heard in the dark mornings that steam and Donna Summers music inspire. His current boyfriend was one of those encounters that seemed to stick. Michael had striking Nordic good looks; tall, athletic, blond, and blue eyes that shimmered like a fjord in the middle of a midnight sun. As an official member of the Sisters of Perpetual Indulgence, Michael was Sister Scandic. He raised significant amounts of money for charity and dropped a few zippers along the way. The Sisters of Perpetual Indulgence is a charity organization born out of the AIDS crisis in the 1980s. Originally, a few gay men dressed up in nuns' habits and solicited money on street corners in San Francisco. The unique character of the group grew into a national organization with strict Catholic initiation practices and demonstrations of organizational skill to raise significant amounts of cash for gay charitable organizations. They are an invaluable asset to the gay community.

The stark reflection of florescent lights paled their already light skins to a sickly translucent pall. As they saw me amble toward them, they smiled their grins, said, "Do we really have to do this?" It was an exploratory dinner that I would never forget.

As we three opened the door, a gust of frying oil slammed into our faces like a Tsunami. The clink and screeching of chairs moving across the linoleum floor, the bubbling fish tank, and the wail of orders being fired to the chefs in the kitchen overwhelmed our senses. As the old woman at the cashier podium waved us to an empty table,

I noticed Leon stumble slightly; he had glanced over at the fish tank, anticipating what he was mandated by his magazine to order. Sitting down, the three of us noted the corral of soy sauce; chili oil; brown hoisin sauce and Chinese mustard huddled at the end of the table. A forest of standing chopsticks and tubs of Asian soupspoons fenced in the little school of additives. Suddenly, with a bang and a slosh, three glasses of clear water landed on the table along with three greasy menus, their nylon stitched bindings frayed from years of handling. The scratched and yellowed lamination over the list of dishes might have been warning us of the adventure or nightmare we were soon to encounter.

"Mmm, 'Special chow mien, with abocado,' I wonder if that's a type of fish?" Michael pondered sarcastically.

Leon rolled his eyes, as I released my own anxiety with a belly laugh. "I wonder if the sushi comes with salsa and guacamole." I continued the bait.

Leon groaned again. With such a weak stomach, I wondered how he landed a job as a restaurant reviewer. As quickly as the water had been splashed down, a post pubescent Asian girl appeared at our table ready to take down our order. We all knew what had to be ordered, we each had made up our mind. Leon pointed awkwardly, hesitantly to the line in the yellow menu that said, "Smiling fish."

Michael ordered the "Special chow mien," and methodically said, "With extra ah-bo-cah-do." The young woman looked at him with dull disdain, like she would at someone with a mental disability.

I pointed to the won ton soup. I knew it was going to be a long night that would end up outside of Club Chop Suey, at the hot dog stand eating Seattle Hot Dogs: grilled onions, cream cheese and BBQ sauce, and wondering if I was sober enough to drive home.

Leon and Michael had purposely seated themselves with their backs to the fish tank, leaving me in full view of the spectacle about to take place. Our waitress handed her order pad with its Chinese script to the man behind the stainless steel bar and then the yelling began.

An old man, maybe the husband of the woman at the cashier's podium, hobbled out of the kitchen, glanced in our direction and smiled, one tooth protruding from his wrinkled grin. He ambled over to the fish tank and plunged his arm up to his elbow into the murky algae waters expertly retrieving a fighting brown-scaled monster that battled for its soon-to-be-extinguished life. Grasping the fish in an iron Chairman Mao fist, goose stepped back into the kitchen, the brown monster valiantly fighting for its life. I caught a quick glimpse of the kitchen, a grease-smeared atmosphere that recalled those deep-fried Twinkies at the Puyallup Fair.

The sounds of chopping, pounding, and sizzling ensued. We three sat agog in our florescent luminescent haze. Michael tried to ease the tension with a tale of how he "encouraged" a new patron to donate money to the Sister's charity fund via his "sisterly" enticements. Leon only stared at the back wall of the restaurant, seemingly oblivious, as if his mind had drifted far out to sea.

Exactly three minutes from the fish being yanked from its algae-clouded home, it flew onto our table. Astonished at the speed of the preparation, I looked down at the full-bodied fish to marvel at the expert presentation.

The young waitress brought the other dishes, family style. She placed large white plates in front of each of us, and then walked off. No acknowledgement of our meal, no questions about any other services desired; it was presumed that we had what we needed and nothing else was to be offered.

I looked across the table at Leon and Michael. Both seemed to have congealed like week-old rice. Their eyes focused on the "Smiling fish" lying on the white serving plate encircled by Ming blue decal designs. At first I didn't notice anything special; the Smiling fish simply looked like any other deep-fried fish, complete with head.

Until it moved.

With full swimming motion, the fins began flailing in its attempt to flee from the plate, the gill flaps and mouth gasping for water and air that it could not breathe because its insides had been gutted with such efficiency and speed that the body and mind had not had time to die. Technically, the fish was still alive, only the essential innards had been removed before it was freshly deep-fried, all but the head. This fish had been swimming and eating its own dinner only moments earlier. My mind immediately flashed on a National Geographic special of lions and zebras, color photos of a zebra desperate to escape a pride of attacking lions but their claws and fangs, brought the zebra down with sheer force, one lion's teeth clamped down like a vise on the zebra's throat as it kicked and withered, being devoured alive.

Now this fish in agony groped for air, swimming in a fake Ming serving plate, and was supposed to gaze as we dined on its body.

Leon was nothing, if not fast, with the agility and speed of a dolphin, he leaped up and plunged out the door onto the brick street, heaving his body over a bike railing, puking his own intestines. I had to admit that the force and volatility with which he projected his disdain was truly inspirational. In all my years on the planet, all the parties, and all the drunken weekends curled around the base of a toilet praying to the porcelain god to spare my life, I had never seen a violent expulsion similar to that. Mike on the other hand remained tofu cold, motionless, his eyes transfixed on the struggling, gasping, freshly fried fish before us. I had seen this same stare from others who had witnessed a horrifying accident and were spellbound by the sheer terror and disbelief.

Leon was experiencing an acute culinary trauma. He reacted with the flight response, while Mike reacted by the freezing. I was angry, in denial of the projected injustice done to the fish. As I looked back to the door Leon had leaped through, the elderly cashier was holding her hand over her mouth in a vain attempt to cover a colossal laugh. Chinese culture maintains that laughing at another's misfortune is impolite. For the Chinese woman, the incident was more akin to watching a scene on America's Funniest Home Video, one she'd seen many times before.

Although the table held several other dishes, only that gasping fish caught our attention. Sensing our disbelief, the waitress slammed down the paper with the indecipherable Chinese characters on the table. That broke the silence. I guessed from the waitress's experience that most people simply rose from the table in a daze and stumbled out the door without paying. This show had been played out before. Michael still stared at the slowly suffocating, disemboweled fish as I kicked him under the table. His eyes met mine and he started to come around. His sarcastic nature returned to the real world, as he sucked in his cheeks and made groping motions with his lips, like the plated fish. The table next to us broke out in an uproar, as they had watched the entire scene with utter fascination. A meaty hand slammed the table like good ol' boys do after a rude joke in a bar. A deep throaty laughter resonated over the linoleum flooring. I turned to see the source of the vibration. Sitting at the table next to ours was a couple, in their late 50's, she was demure, and he was robust. His hands pounded the table again with a sonic force that sloshed our water glasses like waves of a seismic tremor. He was animated and jumping in his seat at the spectacle being played out at our table. His uncut gray hair swayed as he convinced his wife with a forced laughter. I was being subtly manipulated to accept his perception and disembowel my own experience. Comedians do this when they laugh at their own jokes, it forces the audience to accept the joke as funny and question their own sense of the experience. The audience laughs to be part of the joke, never mind that the joke wasn't funny. Only his interpretation and experience were to be acceptable. My focus widened as I surveyed the other members of the audience, and I could see both the look of shock, and acceptance as pounders continued cajoling. Eventually, he had engaged the entire restaurant to accept the performance as part of the experience for the night. Tables pointed, men slapped each other on the back to affirm what the pounder had deduced; everyone was part of our experience and expense.

I looked to the bike rack outside to see if Leon was standing or sitting down from exhaustion. His lunch, breakfast, and probably the yesterday's dinner clotting in the gutter. Leon was as white and translucent as the neon light emanating from Haung Lune.

The dinner ended when Mike stumbled, not quite in control of his body yet, outside to see if Leon was OK, and if he could walk. I followed them down the street after paying for the meal we could not eat. The grandmother cashier handled the transaction with the ambivalence of a jade lion statue cold, translucent, and defiant.

I knew from my relationship with Leon prior to this outing, that he would not want to talk about it. Good old Mormon upbringing would never allow him to dive into the salty lake of shame he knew from growing up.

Afterward, we would pass in the hallways at bars, smile and give excuses about why we had been so unable to make phone calls to keep in touch. A year passed that way.

The experience of the gasping fish lingered in the dark spaces of our minds. In true American form, there is always something new to explore in an open culture. A new sensation sprung on the stage. The country was reminiscing about the "good old days" and trying desperately to reconnect with a time long gone in American culture, the time of good old Common Sense. Corn dogs, marshmallow toasted on a stick, simple pot roasts with potatoes and carrots in a single pot, and Kraft macaroni and cheese became popular again. Sarah Palin the Governor of Alaska entered the American political stage and fueled the desire to return to a folksy sort of bad dream. Through her egotistical "Mama Grizzly Bear" metaphors, she galvanized those disenfranchised Americans that longed for a more isolated America, an America that didn't have to think past their reptilian brain to eat. It was a dangerous time when passions ran high, and brains sank low. Fish sticks outpaced sushi for the first time since the first George Bush presidency.

I returned to Hin Loon recently just to make sure my memory had not forgotten any details. The restaurant had not changed, except the waitress was behind the dinky cashier podium and the fish tank was a little cleaner than I had recalled.

· *We Came Back to Say* ·

MY FEDERAL TRADE COMMISSION TESTIMONY

By Johna Beall

"There may come a day when you must go to the airport as quickly as you can. You get on the next flight to the US, whether you have time to pack your bags or not," my dad warned me quietly.

Then, silence. My mother was in the kitchen making lunch; I was sitting with him chatting. I always gathered information about our business and its history when we were together. He'd been a great teacher. This was a different tone than usual.

"Do you understand?"

I nodded.

In 1991, he'd signed fifty-one percent of the corporation over to me, three years before his death. They also started a life insurance policy for me: for my children really, in case the high murder rate in Colombia left them motherless.

That day in 1991 he'd said, "You have driven me crazy bringing up things I never wanted to talk about. I know you'll be honest when I ask you this. Will you take care of your mother?"

We had worked through a lot of difficult 'stuff' over the years (a technical term). Traveled through it and arrived in a place of peace.

"You know I will, Daddy. You know I love you both. Whatever lifestyle I have, whatever happens, she will be with me."

He picked up his pen, signing fifty-one percent of the corporate shares to me. It was completely unexpected.

He had built the rose farm in 1974, near Bogotá. Asked by Colombians and Dutch partners to start a joint venture: the first rose farm in Colombia. He was a master grower. They had an elevated plateau in the Andes at 8,500 feet above sea level, four degrees north latitude, with twelve hours of sunlight each day, rich volcanic soil. No need to heat the greenhouses, less costly labor, and a good exchange rate from Colombian pesos to dollars.

At the time the farm was built, I was a flower child at UC Berkeley studying Communications, saying to friends: "I'm the only one in the family who knows the meaning of the word 'imperialism'!"

He visited me the last quarter of my senior year, offering me the leadership position in Bogotá. I had minored in Spanish and French. I'd had visions of working in some adventurous business in the Andes wearing gaucho pants and boots. Not the family rose farm! I said no.

Thirteen years later, pregnant with my second child, they asked me again to come back to the family business. I was a psychotherapist in private practice; I had little desire to be involved. They kept asking; I kept saying no. They raised the offer.

Then they leveled with me: funds and roses were disappearing. My dad's health was failing, and his time was limited. They needed help. My eldest sister was working in Colombia and held about thirty percent of the stock in the corporation. She was the heir apparent. They were not sure if it was her, her husband behind her back (marital difficulties), or perhaps someone else on the South American payroll embezzling.

When my sister heard that I had agreed to start, she was happy. We worked together well. Within a year, I had increased sales by fifty percent.

But the news of my ownership of fifty-one percent of the corporate stock three years later enraged her.

A week later, she was unavailable for our calls to the farm. We asked her staff where she had gone. "She has taken a long weekend off, how can we help?" She showed up at the office with no warning, fresh off an overnight flight.

"I will buy you out," she said to me without hesitation.

That answered our question. The company was already hers (in her mind), and she had cash. My dad walked out of the room saying, "You two work it out." His constitution was too weak.

"Will you take care of mother?" I asked. "I've promised to care for her."

"No!" she said. "She can rot."

Mother put her face in her hands. We were both stunned. She was this angry at our parents? Her words echoed in the room, I'll never forget.

"If you won't work with me, together, we'll need to buy you out," I stammered. We negotiated for quite some time, all the details, including time payments. That was the last time I spoke with her.

In April 1994, after a painful decline, my dad died. That September, while grieving, I was awarded the Blue Chip Enterprise Award by Washington State Chamber of Commerce for problem solving in business. But the challenges kept coming. Cheap roses sold by competitors. Thrips arrived with a shipment of rose plants from Bakersfield, a terrible plague to roses. Excessive boron in the soil. An infestation of Nematodes.

When the Federal Trade Commission imposed a thirty-five-cent-per-rose tariff on all imported roses from Colombia into the US, that was worse. It was an 'Anti-Dumping' action, instigated by struggling North American rose growers.

Our farm was wholly US-owned: established when North Americans could start a business in Colombia. The farm was run efficiently, as Daddy had always run his Palo Alto rose-growing operation, where I'd grown up working weekends and summers as a freckle-faced kid. Every box custom packed for wholesale florists across the US: they paid high prices for gorgeous vibrant colors and rich, deep reds, long stems. When I visited our customers around the US, I'd seen on their fresh-cut price sheets:

Bulk roses: $.30 Beall's Roses: $.70

Other rose growers in Colombia and Ecuador sent hundreds of boxes of roses to Miami daily on consignment. Boxes that went for four to ten cents per rose. These are the roses you see in grocery stores, "bucket roses." We were penalized by the FTC in the same way as these other growers who dumped mass quantities of roses into US markets. Our prices ranged from twenty-eight to forty-eight cents per rose, direct sales, not consignment.

The FTC allotted seven minutes for our appeal regarding this tariff.

For 105 years, five generations of our Scottish clan grew roses, starting first on Vashon Island. In 1889, the family began growing flowers and vegetables on the island, bringing the fresh produce by boat to sell at Seattle's Pike Place Market. During the depression, they sold more vegetables, and with hard work kept it going over the years. After WWII, they expanded to Palo Alto and then moved to Bogotá. By 1994, we exported over six million premium roses annually to Europe and US markets.

From this broken family, I emerged, searching. Seeking clarity and peace, love and beauty. I somehow thought rose growers might share the love of beauty.

I flew 2,211 miles from Vashon Island to Washington, DC to testify. Our sales office was still on the island. The Vashon farm run by my cousin had already closed.

We stay in downtown Washington DC. I awaken early and shower in silence the day of my testimony. I wrap my carefully polished nails and long fingers around the silky stockings, pulling the thin pale pantyhose up my right foot first, over pointed, pale pink lacquered toenails, then toes, my arches, up thin bony ankles. Working on staying calm, feeling the touch of the smooth stockings over my calf muscles, pulling up over knee and savoring the feeling of the stretchy fabric coming up my thigh. Deep breathing: relaxing into my femininity, my strong body. Raised on a farm after all—albeit a rose farm in Palo Alto.

My left foot then, slowly, sensing my foot and ankle. Remembering a friend saying to me before I left, "So ironic that a woman is sent to give the testimony, after all the misogyny in the family." It had always been a patriarchy until it came to my generation. Here I was, the youngest of four daughters, the last one left in the business.

"How does one prepare to testify before the Federal Trade Commission?" I'd mused to friends.

"We'll polish the statement in advance," our attorney had said. "I'll prep you in person the day before, when you arrive in DC. You'll do fine."

Not wanting to wake the kids or my mom, who was there to help with them in the room adjoining, I moved silently. Everyone was tired from seeing the Smithsonian the day before. We'd made arrangements to see the White House the following day. For the morning, each of the kids would be coloring their favorite thing at the museums, and writing reports for their schools while I go to the Department of Commerce.

"What does one wear to make a statement at the DOC?" I'd joked with another girlfriend.

I slip on the tight Navy blue knit skirt, navy heels. Pulling over my head the matching navy knit top, I smile to myself. Conservative-appearing, my two-piece navy dress was made in Italy for Victoria's Secret. I pull the skirt down a bit, not so short. My long, red, wool coat is hanging near the door. I focus on the details to stay grounded and calm. I check to see that my briefcase is ready, next to my coat.

For forty-two years I've done my best imitation of a son; I'm named for dad. "The smart one," my sisters referred to me. "Her dad's last chance for a namesake," Momma always said.

Brushing my shoulder-length blonde hair, I gather it into a ponytail. Simple gold earrings, gold watch, no wedding ring, just a Colombian emerald ring on my right hand. I finish my makeup, still trying to relax. A sip of tea made in the pot in the room. This morning I have not been able to eat, though I should. No caffeine, my nerves running wild already.

Dressed, I slip out quietly. I descend. In the lobby I ask the concierge to call a cab. First stop, the company's attorney's office. He and I will ride together to the Trade Commission.

"Several out front, Miss."

"Great. Thanks." I walk through the lobby, where the smell of coffee and bacon turns my stomach. I withdraw quickly from the smell of grease on a griddle, heading to the glass doors facing the busy street outside.

"God help me," I say to myself, feeling very alone.

"God's will be done," My mother had said to me. We knew this day was crucial to the future of our business.

I step across the threshold, passing through that point between the sliding doors that open before me into the nation's capital. Advancing to the head of the line of cabbies waiting in December morning mist. A gracious, dark-skinned cabbie nods and smiles at me, opening the rear door. I give him the address; he starts the meter. I am grateful for his kindness—the warmest greeting I will get all day. We proceed to the Capital.

· *Johna Beall* ·

For some reason, the first movement of Beethoven's 5th Symphony is stuck in my mind. I sit nervously in the rear of the cab, watching grey boxes in a row; squares and oblongs line every block. It's the government sector. Monotonous grey rectangles, with rows of identical windows, symmetrical, consistent buildings. We stop before a glass-paned office building just beyond the grey rectangles. Our corporate attorney, Chip, is waiting and jumps in the other side of the cab.

"Right on time!" he says cheerfully.

Next stop, the FTC. Etched in stone across the top of the building: Department of Commerce.

We stop, Chip pays the driver.

Inside we walk, riding up in the colorless steel elevator to drab hallways with identical doors all down the row. The designated room is stark white with grey, metal furnishings. The American flag and President Clinton's photo suffice to decorate the room, where forty or fifty of us rose growers and attorneys congregate.

My testimony is the last of the morning on this day I will never forget. Heightened awareness at every step. Time racing, yet taking forever.

Seven minutes.

After 105 years growing flowers and food for five generations, I've traveled 2,320 miles from Vashon to Washington, DC to respond to the Federal Trade Commission for our appeal. We've been paying the thirty-five-cent tariff per rose for three months. Our business is already in trouble. Our farm is the only wholly US-owned flower business in Colombia. Impossible by definition to be dumping since profits came to the US.

At one point earlier, I'd received a letter from Chip: "Send a ten-thousand-dollar retainer to my friend Jay in Philadelphia, and he will arrange a lunch with Ron Brown." (Secretary of Commerce for Clinton). It was beyond our scope; we had already spent 17,000 dollars on our defense. Our cash flow was drained by the tariffs. Was my interpretation of this offer incorrect? I'll never know. I followed dad's advice: "Never succumb to requests for cash to bend rules. Follow the letter of the law, despite offers otherwise." We had filed an appeal like all the other, much-larger farms with deeper pockets.

We are all seated in a square, chairs up against the walls of the stale room, somber, serious.

A few other statements precede mine. Colombian men in grey and black elegant wool suits, overcoats, white shirts, nondescript ties. Few acknowledge me; I'm the foreigner, the North American grower.

The entire room resembles a sea of grey. Finally, I hear the words, "Beall's Roses come forward."

From the back wall where we are waiting, we walk, Chip at my side. We sit at the L-shaped table, addressing the panel of commissioners facing us at the front of the room, a long, stark, metal desk. Two women and three men, all middle-aged or older, in grey suits, ashen, stoic.

I pull the microphone toward me, placing my hands flat on either side of my three double-spaced pages. I read with feeling about our business model, finishing with, "We are not dumping roses into North American markets."

The review board calls for lunch recess.

We put on our overcoats as the crowd exits. Surprisingly, one of the grey-suited commissioners approaches me and begins to speak. "I'm sorry, Ms. Beall, that your farm will be a casualty of this action. This is about something much bigger."

My mouth falls open. I cannot speak.

Chip takes my elbow and pulls. He nods, acknowledging the commissioner while he pulls me to the exit. My mouth is still open.

We descend in an elevator jammed with other rose growers and their attorneys in silence. Chip hails a cab and turns to me as we ride back to the Marriot.

"She doesn't understand what she's saying. She doesn't grasp the history of your family, the legacy, the one hundred-plus years of hard work. She doesn't get it. I'm sorry, Johna."

After that, we rode in silence. Exhausted from the tension and anticipation, devastated by her comment, I was running on empty.

"I'll be in touch as soon as I hear from the Review Board, Johna. Take care of yourself and your mother." Chip stood up as I got out the other side of the cab. He waved goodbye over the cab. I headed back, grateful for my sweet, loving family.

Two weeks later, the confirmation came through: "Appeal denied." Several of the large farms did have their appeal accepted. They had more attorneys, more time granted to testify, more cash on hand to make the appropriate influences. We were given no explanation for why others did win their appeal, while ours was denied. Their business model was not like ours, they were sending in large numbers of cut roses at low prices, and yet somehow their appeal was honored.

Seven minutes! After 105 years.

From September to the end of March, the DOC continued to levy the thirty-five-cent tariff on every rose we imported. By that March, all but twenty-five percent of our regular orders had been cancelled. The tariff was the final blow to our business.

The Wholesale Florists and Florist Suppliers of America filed a suit against the DOC and won their case later that year. The tariff was eliminated after ten months. For us, it was too late. In June 1995, we closed the doors on our North American operation.

My last trip to the farm, in early May to check the Mother's Day crop, I knew was my last. I took home my most prized possessions from our home on the farm. I made sure my Colombian partner, Benito, had access to all the information he needed to carry on.

Summer is the lean season in the rose business, when people grow their own roses in their gardens. Benito would have to make it on his own with the farm in the future. We would be receiving the accounts receivable in the US through the end May. Those funds went to care for my mother, who lived another thirteen years. She lived with us as long as possible and then in a small, private home with twenty-four-hour nurses, with four other residents. We remained close; she was coherent, we visited daily. The night she died I sat holding her hand, softly singing one of her favorite hymns to her, over and over.

In those last several years, I traveled 4,111 miles monthly between Vashon and Bogotá to supervise farm operations and North American sales. I'd done my best to keep it going.

I could have had lunch with Ron Brown for 10,000 dollars.

Ron Brown actually was killed in a mysterious plane crash into a mountainside in Croatia on April 3, 1996. The crash remained unexplained for a time. I always wondered: had he made *such* enemies? "The final Air Force Investigation attributed the crash to pilot error and a poorly designed landing approach." There were no survivors of that tragic incident.

At the Vashon Cemetery entrance stands the grey Beall headstone, which reads: "Seek Ye First the Kingdom of God". Yes.

Each in our own way.

FINDING DON CAMERON

By Sue Wiedenfeld

A FEW YEARS AGO, I BEGAN WRITING about what I imagined had happened just before I was conceived at a party where my eighteen-year-old mother was drinking with fellow college students. I described the setting in a large, old home where the parents were out of town, and the eighteen-to-twenty-year-olds had the place to themselves to dance and party. Sounds of "Jailhouse Rock" and "Great Balls of Fire" covered the quiet retreat of couples as they sought privacy. In my fantasy, they all eventually intertwined in pairs, clothing loosening and then dropping away as music echoed from the empty living room. My mother said, "Everyone was doing it," as she explained having sex with a man she barely knew.

I found my mother, Phebe, through a psychic, twenty-seven-and-a-half years ago. These years, her mind has become clouded by dementia and is worsening daily, preventing me from getting any more information about what happened fifty-eight years ago. Yet I have wanted to find out more about this man who was my biological father. At times I have berated myself for not asking Phebe more about my father when she was still vibrant and coherent. During most of the time I have known Phebe, I felt and acted as if it only mattered for me to know my mother. It was as if we tacitly agreed to a protective silence; a silence suggesting that I didn't even need to have a father. It was as if he were only an "extra" in the story. There was awkwardness, too, as I was aware she barely knew him. Perhaps I didn't want to make her uncomfortable by having her admit, again, that she didn't know him, this man whose child she bore. With time, it became clearer to me that her original description that he was "in her group" may have been an exaggeration. Perhaps she only "knew" him that one evening, the night of the party, blurred by a veil of alcohol. In the conversations we did have, she was matter-of-fact. She said my father was in the same year as she was in school, though older because he had been in the military.

"Your father's name is Don Cameron," she told me in our very first conversation. From my adoption agency birth record and Phebe's recollection, I also knew my father was one of eight children. I knew his approximate age, and I knew that he had served in the Marines before going to college. Also, I had a physical description of him: About six feet tall, hazel/green eyes, and a thick neck, like a football player's. In an earlier effort to find him, I had gotten photos from the 1953 Greeley College yearbook and I could not find a Don Cameron in it, which seemed odd.

My own son has piercing green eyes. He has long, thin toes and a beautiful singing voice. None of these characteristics are in my biological mother's family or in my husband's family. Sometimes I have looked into his eyes and said, "Those must be Don Cameron's eyes," or "Well, I don't know about those long, funny toes, they must be Don Cameron's." Or, "That beautiful singing voice must have come from Don Cameron." My husband and I have joked about anything in my son that we don't recognize, but for me, the joking has been driven by my deep yearning to know more about my father.

My son's growing up has deepened and intensified my desire to find my father. I am fully aware of the life expectancy for men—around seventy-six years, just about the age my father would be. Perhaps this added to my feeling of urgency that Father's Day, 2011. I woke up feeling compelled to resume my search for my father. As I wrote about my biological parents, I had begun to feel certain that my father had lived close to the college. Most families with eight children do not send them away to college; surely he had lived in a nearby town. Because of this conviction, I decided to call Steve, the background researcher an attorney friend had recommended to me. Perhaps he could search Colorado, where my mother went to school and where they had met.

When I called Steve in the late afternoon of Father's Day, to my surprise, he answered. He listened openly to my persuasive case that we should search for Don Cameron in Colorado. After hearing everything I knew, he sounded optimistic.

"I will work on this tomorrow and get back to you," he said.

I was encouraged. I can only say, as I had begun writing vivid descriptions of the circumstances of my conception, I had begun to believe them.

❖

The next evening at about 7:20, Steve called. He had found a Don Cameron, exactly the right age, who had lived in Loveland in the 1950s, twenty minutes from my mother's college in Greeley, Colorado. One of eight children, he had served in the Marines and fit the description I had been given. My heart leaped as he continued to list the relatives he had uncovered in Colorado, Oregon, and Nevada. I was writing furiously to record every word he said. There was a pause. And then Steve said, "Unfortunately, Don died in February of last year."

Too late! was all I could think. As I had feared, my chance to meet my father was over. Why had I not pursued this sooner?

I was caught between my excitement of finally finding him and the stunning thought that I would never meet HIM, only his family. I felt surrounded by a tangle of happiness and sadness, as if lost in a maze. But I also felt some exhilaration. After all these years, he had existed!

Steve gave me the names of two people who appeared to be his brothers, as well as his recent wife and other relatives. I waited a few days, letting my heart begin to open to this new family. Could this be? Could my searching be over at last? There was no rush to call since he was dead, the very fear that had propelled me to resume my search on Father's Day.

How would I introduce myself, fifty-eight years later? Who would I tell the family I was? What if they didn't know about me? What if they didn't believe me? What if they wouldn't talk to me at all? Who should contact the family, Steve or I? In the end, I decided I would contact them. I told myself I wanted medical information. That's what I would tell them, too.

Over the following days, I realized it was much more than medical information that I wanted. I wanted every second of interaction with them that I could have. If this was my family, I didn't want to miss a minute. I had already missed my father's entire life.

A few days passed before I worked up the nerve to call the number listed for the woman who had been my father's last wife. She was abrupt.

"Hello."

"Hello, my name is Sue, and I am calling about your husband, Don Cameron, who I know has died. I think I am related to him."

"What is your name?"

"Sue Wiedenfeld."

She coldly stated, "There are no Sue's in the family. I can't help you."

When she was so dismissive, the desperate part of me that had searched so long for my father felt like screaming at her, "I am telling you I am related, and that would mean there *is* a 'Sue' in your family!"

"Thank you," I said quietly and hung up, stunned by both her stupidity and her rudeness, feeling like a sea anemone who had just been poked. I retreated inside. This was not a very auspicious start to contacting my father's family. I needed time to recover before trying anyone else.

I waited a few more days, and then decided to call the oldest brother. A woman answered, and I asked for "Joe Cameron."

She said, "He is not here right now; he is at the casino and will be back in about an hour. Can I help you?" She was warm and sounded kind. Dare I ask her?

"Maybe I should talk to you…." I said haltingly.

She was quiet, invitingly quiet, so I jumped in. "Your husband is listed as a brother to Don Cameron, who I know died last year in February. I think I am his daughter."

She was interested and curious. "I am Joe's wife, Kathy. Can you tell me more about this?"

She listened kindly as I recounted my story. She gently encouraged me as she heard me describe my father as one of eight children, in the Marines, and as possibly having green or hazel eyes.

"I can understand your wanting to find him," she said.

All of what I said was true of her deceased brother-in-law. All of it was true of this man named Don Cameron, the name of my father.

· *We Came Back to Say* ·

"My husband will want to talk to you. Can you call back in a little while? Don never had kids, so if you are his daughter, it would make the whole family very happy."

I called back. Her husband was suspicious.

"I would expect one of my other brothers to have a child I didn't know about, but not Don. Don wasn't that way. What makes you think he is your father?"

I repeated the facts.

"I have to find those papers from his time in the service. I am not sure he was around when your mother got pregnant. It just wasn't like him. He wasn't that good with the ladies."

A few days later, Joe's daughter, Shirleen, called me. She was warm and very friendly, but told me her father wasn't sure what to think about me. She went on to tell me many stories about the family. Secrets about who had mental illness, who had been pregnant when they had gotten married. She told me how difficult it had been for the family when Don's father died, leaving eight children. Don had been only twelve, but he began functioning like the head of the family, having to work to support the family instead of going to college. Shirleen was kind and disclosing, as a cousin might be. She gave me the "insider" information. I was grateful. She described her father as a suspicious person and suggested I give him time. She told me how much my father had been respected in the family and how much he had wanted to have children. She suggested I call another brother, Jim.

Jim was clear, insisting "If Don had known your mother was pregnant, he would have married her. He couldn't have known. He was the patriarch of the family after our father died. Everyone wanted him to have kids—he just never did. Instead, he lived with our mother." Both he and his wife, Terry, were open-hearted and welcoming. She even said, "We would be very happy to have you as part of this family."

Her words warmed my heart. I could feel a wrenching hole inside of me beginning to fill with everything I was coming to know about this man.

My mother, Phebe, had told me that Don Cameron, "never came forward." She had assumed her roommate Marty's boyfriend would have told Don that Phebe had gotten pregnant that night. Phebe said she never knew for sure if Don had ever found out about the pregnancy.

A few things didn't add up. The adoption papers said that Don was in college while the family said he couldn't go to college as he needed to work to support his family. The papers also said he played guitar and basketball. The family said he did neither. These disparities made me slightly hesitant. Yet so much was a perfect fit. What were the chances of the name, age, number of siblings, being in the Marines, and living nearby being wrong?

Years ago, I tracked down Phebe's college roommate. So I called Marty to ask her, once again, if she could remember any more about Don Cameron. Did she, by chance, recall *anything* Phebe had said about this man? Marty had gotten engaged about the same time that Phebe had become pregnant, and her excitement for planning her wedding and the fifty-eight years that had passed eclipsed any memories of these details in Phebe's life. They had taken a road trip together for Phebe to tell her parents she was pregnant. I was hoping Marty might recall something from the conversations over those many long miles, yet she remembered nothing. Marty was apologetic.

What she did tell me, more directly this time, is that this was a man Phebe did not know well at all. It was essentially a one-night stand. She also suggested that Phebe may have made up interesting details so, as she was being interviewed at the home for unwed mothers, it would seem she knew him better than she did. This would prove to her mother that Don had been her boyfriend.

About this time, Jim and Terry sent me photos of Don Cameron. I pored over them, taking in every detail of each one. I saw the eyes in these photos—the eyes that I had been telling my son were Don Cameron's. Almost reverently, I cut a rectangular shape out of a piece of paper that exposed just Don's eyes so that I could see the eyes alone. It was striking. They were identical to my son's.

I could feel a deep wound I had carried most of my life beginning to heal. I loved the connections with these people. I felt woven in the warm and comfortable web of this big, Catholic family. I could even accept that, if I couldn't know my father, this was his family, whom I *could* know. They felt familiar. I would take in all I could as I enjoyed the feeling of coming home. Though tentative at first, a deep and stirring connection began to come alive in me.

· *We Came Back to Say* ·

When Jim called to let me hear a CD Don had sent him years before, I was at a shopping center. I sat down at a sidewalk café to hear the moving story, the only time I would hear my father's voice, of an escapade he had at work, when he was threatened by an armed robber and had to follow the nerve-wracking instructions. His voice was soothing as he told the details. Strong. Lovely. Gentle. I could imagine the big, inviting body I had seen in pictures and could imagine being welcomed into his arms. I savored every sweet word. The sound of his voice seemed to sink into every pore of my body.

Shirleen and I agreed that her dad, Joe, would most likely be convinced by DNA testing. It seemed a small price for claiming my family, and it would settle any doubts.

The brothers readily agreed to DNA testing and the saliva samples were sent in. The testing took about a week. The week flew by as I waited, excited to get the results. I got the call from the testing center in my car.

"We will be sending you the results by fax today."

"Can you give me the results?"

"No, for privacy reasons, I have to fax them."

"Are they conclusive?"

"Yes, absolutely."

"Then, no one could argue about them?"

"No."

My spirits soared. I had feared equivocal results that would leave doubt. I felt light as a feather as I hurried home, my heart racing. I noticed nothing as I sped across the Montlake Bridge to my neighborhood, my home, and the papers in my fax machine. To the end of my search.

I ran in, grabbed the papers, and flopped into a chair to read the results: Ninety-eight percent certain. Thank God.

Then I saw it.

Ninety-eight percent certain that we *weren't* related.

I had been so sure. I had been positive that certain results meant we were related. I couldn't believe what I was reading. Stunned, I called the lab, and they reassured me the only way for false results to occur was if the brothers hadn't sent in their saliva, and if it had been someone else's. I still didn't believe the results, but now I felt helpless to

136

prove he was my father. It was DNA vs. my heart. I wanted to believe my heart. And I wanted science to prove it.

Six months have passed. I now accept that the DNA test showed he wasn't my father. But before I sent the pictures back to the family, I copied every single one. I cherish them. A part of me can't let go of feeling this man *was* my father. I wanted this family and they wanted me. I wanted the storybook ending. So did they. Yet, somehow, through this experience, something did settle in me. I am not fully resolved, but I find I don't have much energy to search for another Don Cameron.

In my heart, I feel I have already found him.

A COSMIC SHIFT IN UTAH
By Robyne L. Curry

"How'd you get to Wasatch, Robyne?" Marquetta asked.

The question hung in the air as I looked around at eyes looking at me, waiting to hear how once upon a time a fourteen-year-old black kid from Cleveland, Ohio, had found her way to central Utah to attend a Presbyterian-affiliated, college-prep boarding school smack-dab in the middle of Mormon country.

Not your typical high school experience. But then, Wasatch Academy was not a typical high school. Certainly not like those posh East Coast, old-school-tie prep schools. For starters, Wasatch was co-ed, and its students—white, black, Native American, African, Middle Eastern, Thai—couldn't have been more diverse, nor could their reasons for attending. Like Jill, my roommate who, because she lived in Yosemite National Park, where the nearest high school was more than 50 miles away, attended Wasatch just like her brother had before her. Or Joanne, whose newly married father and stepmother wanted to begin their union without four teenagers underfoot and so dispatched their Brady Bunch off to Wasatch. Or Pat, who lived in Nicaragua thanks to her mining-engineer father and was the third in a line of red-headed siblings sent stateside for high school: all to Wasatch.

That I recall this about my classmates made it hard to believe that it'd been forty years since graduation. But there we were, thirteen members of the class of '72, fresh from a reunion dinner heavy on picture taking, picture sharing (*pass the camera so I can see Joanne's grandkids*), and a little white-lying (*OMG, you look so-o-o good!*), sitting in an L-shaped alcove in a hotel bar, sipping wine or whiskey and doing what we'd traveled miles and years to do: reflect, reminisce, reconnect.

· *Robyne L. Curry* ·

"How'd you get to Wasatch, Robyne?"

❖

"Do you have everything you need in there?" my mother asked, watching me stuff the last of my personal items, sheets, towels, and winter clothing into a seemingly bottomless trunk bound for Mount Pleasant, Utah, barely two weeks before the start of school. The pick-up men were due any second and I was still packing.

"I think I have everything on the list," I said, checking the inventory of suggested items sent to new students. "If not, we can just pack the rest in our suitcases and take it with us on the plane."

"Our suitcases?" My mother laughed. "Huh! You'd better have everything you need in that trunk, young lady, 'cuz I'm not carrying anything extra."

She was joking of course. She'd have carried ten suitcases on her back if she had to. That's what mothers do. Luckily for her, the freight haulers arrived and collected the massive trunk, placing it on a truck that would take it to a train that would transport it 2,000 miles west to Wasatch Academy. In two weeks' time I would travel those same 2,000 miles, carried by plane, bus and youthful exuberance.

With its Rocky Mountain locale and international student body, Wasatch Academy seemed the world to me, and I was eager to go. I'd found the school in the back of a magazine, just a tiny ad on a page of similar notices for fat camps and music camps and ways to earn extra money in your spare time. I'm not sure why I sent for a brochure, since I figured my mother would never let me go that far, even though the ad made the school seem charming and accessible.

But in 1968 America was changing. The country was embracing the idea of righting racial inequities which brought new opportunities for blacks in jobs, housing and education. Wasatch Academy, with a student body resembling a mini United Nations, seemed a perfect fit for the times and my inquisitive nature. Perhaps more than anything the idea of going away to school fueled my wanderlust, already in overdrive though I'd been absolutely nowhere.

When the school's thick packet of information arrived, I was like a puppy with a new shoe, unable to put it down.

"What's this?" my mother asked, eyeing the brochure, a four-panel flyer studded with sepia images of stately brick buildings, smiling students, concerned-looking faculty.

"It's a catalog to Wasatch Academy," I said. "It's a college-prep boarding school that's co-ed. You always said if I went to a private school it would have to be co-ed."

"Uh-huh. And where is this Wasatch Academy?"

"It's, uh, in, uh, uh, Utah ... Mount Pleasant, Utah."

"Excuse me?"

My mother wasn't exactly keen on the idea of me leaving the nest. Like most women of her generation, she'd wanted nothing more than to be a wife and mother. But fate had other plans. Her marriage to my father had ended after ten years, during which she'd miscarried more than once; I was the only child. Life wasn't easy for a single mother in the '50s and '60s, but she loved the job and wasn't ready to relinquish the reins. On the other hand, she believed education was the key to a better life, so putting aside her maternal desires to give me that shot was a no-brainer.

Of course, I had no idea the kind of sacrifice I was asking of her. At fourteen, my world still pretty much revolved around me, and all I could think about were the things I would see and the people I would meet and the adventures I would have. Who and what I'd be leaving behind never entered my mind.

"I know Utah's a little far," I said, blind to understatement. "But can I apply? I mean, it wouldn't hurt to apply. And they probably won't accept me anyway."

But something told me they would.

And why not? I was a top student in the top track of a junior high whose administrators worked hard to place promising students in private schools.

And so it was after weeks and rounds of paperwork—filling out application forms, getting school transcripts, securing teachers' recommendations, having my mother lay bare her financial condition—that another thick, white envelope with a by now familiar logo arrived bearing the news: "Dear Robyne, We are pleased to welcome you to the freshman class of Wasatch Academy for the 1968-1969 academic year."

Robyne L. Curry

"Mommy, Mommy, I got in, I got in!" I screamed. "And look, I got practically a full scholarship!"

"Let me see that," my mother said, reaching for the acceptance letter. A glimmer of pride flashed as she scanned the words. She may not have wanted me to go, but the die was cast, and she delighted in my achievement.

"Well, I guess we're going to Utah."

"We?"

"Oh yeah. You don't think I'd let you go out there all by yourself, do you? We don't know anything about these people except what we read here. For all I know there might not even be a Wasatch Academy. You bet I'm going out there. I'm gonna make sure there really *is* a school out there."

Which is why barely two weeks before the start of school we were feverishly packing a bottomless pit of a trunk bound for Mount Pleasant, Utah. The pick-up men were due any second and we weren't ready. How do you pack for a cosmic shift in life?

❖

In 1968, the Continental Trailways bus to Mount Pleasant, Utah, left Salt Lake City at 6:30 p.m. My mother, a stickler for punctuality, made sure we were at the station in plenty of time. Two hours early. The waiting room was hot and stuffy in an era before widespread air-conditioning, but at least it was clean and not terribly dingy. There was a photo booth on one wall where twenty-five cents bought a strip of four black-and-white poses. I would have hopped in to capture the moment for time immemorial except that my mother and I had done just that the day before in a five-and-dime in downtown Salt Lake. Aside from trying to catch a cooling breeze from the room's only fan, an oscillating type mounted high in a corner, there was little else to do but wait—and swipe at a fly buzzing past my face.

By 6:00 p.m., the sleepy terminal had started to hum with the energy of fresh-faced teenagers arriving with suitcases and knapsacks and guitar cases. (I think one even had a peace symbol on it.) Many of the kids knew each other and echoes of, "hey, how was your summer?" bounced around the room. Part of me wanted to get up and introduce myself to somebody, anybody. But I was too shy. Instead, I sat glued to my hard plastic seat and watched as the room grew thick with kids like me all headed, I was certain, to Wasatch Academy.

It was nearly 10:00 p.m. when the bus finally pulled into Mount Pleasant and onto campus. Turns out the 6:30 bus was a milk run, stopping often enough to turn 100 miles into a real three-hour tour. Almost immediately kids spilled from the bus, their pent-up adolescent energy erupting in hoots and hollers that quickly put an end to the silent night. Faculty and students already back on campus heard the commotion and rushed out to meet the bus. Everybody was so happy to see everybody, they all said, even the two people who stood out like sore thumbs: my mother and me, the only parent-child combo in the mix.

Amid this happy pandemonium my mother managed to snag a boy we'd seen on the bus and asked where we might find Finks Dorm, home to freshman and sophomore girls. He pointed to a friendly-looking, three-story, late-Victorian brick house with a wide front porch standing practically behind us. He grabbed a couple of our bags and started walking. We followed. With our remaining suitcases in tow, we wrestled the lot down a short walkway, up the porch steps and through the front door.

"Hello, you must be Robyne Curry," said a petite pistol of a woman, fiftyish, with Betty Grable legs who rushed over to greet us. I was amazed that she seemed to know me.

"Yes ... I am ... and this is my mother, Helyn Curry."

"Mrs. Curry, I'm so glad to meet you," she said, pumping my mother's hand. "I'm Mildred Robson, I'm the dorm mother, and we're just thrilled to have Robyne here with us at Wasatch."

"Thank you," my mother smiled.

After more pleasantries, Mrs. Robson called over to a group of girls watching TV in the lounge behind us and made a quick round of introductions. She then led us out of the vestibule and down a brief corridor to my room. Bare and undecorated, dorm rooms look sad at the beginning of a school year—particularly at night. Perhaps reading between the worry lines on my mother's face, Mrs. Robson realized that now would be a good time to sing the school's praises. A newbie herself, she understood the doubts and second guesses that could toy with a parent's mind and knew how to address them. Part diplomat, part saleswoman, part psychologist, Mrs. Robson put my mother completely at ease with her reassuring patter. Until that fateful question.

"*Where are you staying?*"

We were such rubes, my mother and I, and I mean that in the nicest, purest sense of the word. We had our virtues, but travel savvy we were not. We'd successfully navigated our first plane trip anywhere, from Cleveland to Salt Lake City, and then managed that bus leg down to Mount Pleasant. But when Mrs. Robson innocently asked where my mother would be staying, we were unmasked as the naïfs we were.

"Uh, well, um, I was hoping there'd be a hotel nearby," my mother sputtered, "or maybe a spare room somewhere?"

The only hostelry in Mount Pleasant, Utah (pop. ca. 2,500), was a motel-café-and-gas-station near the edge of town that still looked like it had on the front of a 1940s picture postcard—only the gas station was changed. Without a car, the motel was out of the question. Plus, with students returning all weekend its ten or so rooms would have been booked anyway. Fortunately, Finks had a third floor that was not being used that year, so Mrs. Robson offered my mother a room there. It wasn't the Ritz, but it was handy, the price was right, and its creature comforts were the same as mine would be. Whatever fears my mother might have had about leaving me at Wasatch, Mrs. Robson was single-handedly beginning to erase.

The next day campus fully sprang to life as more students returned. My roommate Jill arrived, accompanied by her father, the postmaster at Yosemite, and her mother, whose care packages of cream-cheese brownies still linger in my memory. She offered to drive Jill and me and my mother to the Penney's on Main Street to buy stuff for our room. We bought matching black-and-orange plaid bedspreads that instantly transformed our room. But I was nervous about this impromptu shopping trip because whereas Jill's parents were solidly middle class, my mother was a junior high school library assistant and I fretted about straining her pink collar budget. But if this purchase was a hardship for her, she never let on.

The rest of the weekend proceeded much as one would expect. I registered for classes, bought my books—I even auditioned for the choir. Once my mother told the music director that she'd be more than happy to pack and ship my French horn, I became an instant member of the band, too.

At the end of the weekend, with all the back-to-school ceremonies wrapped up, students began to settle down and prepare for the first day of class; parents were long gone. Except mine.

The bus to Salt Lake City came through Mount Pleasant just once a day, at 5:00 a.m. Because we didn't know this ahead of time my mother was still around. Frankly, I was glad to have her. Throughout the weekend she'd been my trusty companion as we scoured the campus, meeting faculty and staff who always mentioned how happy they were to have me enrolled and who treated her with great respect. She'd been a fierce mama bear sizing up Mount Pleasant and its citizenry to make sure her cub would feel at home there. Except for me peeling off to join in a freshman mixer on the football field, the two of us had done everything together. I'd relied on her, depended on her, and only now, on the eve of the first day of school, did it dawn on me that I wasn't in Cleveland anymore.

Adolescence is such a funny age. You want your parents to give you space *and* be within arm's reach, just in case you need money or a ride or—heaven forbid!—advice. Going to Wasatch was all my idea; no one forced me into it. It was to be my big adventure, a chance to meet new people and do new things. I knew my new classmates would be white and not black, but I was hungry to experience life. It would be exciting. It would be fun. I never dreamed it would hurt.

Shortly before lights out I made a final ascent to Finks' third floor. My mother would be on that 5:00 a.m. bus next day so I wouldn't see her again until Christmas. This was goodbye.

"Well, I guess this is it," I said. "It was a good weekend, huh?"

"Yes, it was," she seconded. "These are nice people here, Robyne. I'm not worried about you; you're in good hands, you'll be all right. But don't forget to call me every Sunday, you hear? Collect."

"I will," I promised.

We exchanged more small talk, delaying the inevitable.

"How are you going to wake up in time for the bus?" I asked.

"Mrs. Robson lent me an alarm clock."

"Oh, OK. Well, the riser here rings at 6:30 in the morning. Can you believe that? I never had to get up that early before. I guess I'd better go now."

We embraced a last time, and then I left.

"You be good," my mother called out, one last reminder.

On the way back to my room, with a lump growing in my throat, eyes beginning to sting, it finally hit me: *I'm on my own now.*

Years later I wondered if my mother had had the same epiphany as she rode out of town. I can only imagine the bittersweet mix of joy and sorrow running through her as she gazed through a window onto the passing countryside, realizing that part of her job as a mother was done, and hoping against hope that she'd got it right.

❖

"Wow, I never knew that about you, Robyne," Marquetta said.

"You were pretty brave to do that all by yourself, without really knowing anything about Wasatch," Joanne added. "At least I had Betty and Carol and Steve."

"Brave? Oh I don't know," I countered.

It's true. After forty years watching people do a double take whenever I mention having gone to high school in Utah (*huh?*), I still think of myself as just a fourteen-year-old kid with a head full of dreams, a desire to see the world, and a mother who gave me an incredible gift when she let me go. I think there are probably a million stories like mine. There have to be. Because Wasatch Academy is a place where kids of all kind come from all over the globe, leaving home for probably the first time in their lives, and converge in a tiny town in the middle of Utah where a world of amazing possibilities opens up to them. Who doesn't have a story to tell?

THE COOKIE SCHOLARSHIP
By Jean Engler

THE COOKIE SCHOLARSHIP WAS PART OF A LONG TRADITION of gift giving in our family. Jack and Wilma were creative gift givers, most often from necessity. Wilma always felt bad that she couldn't purchase whatever gift she wanted for her children and her grandchildren, and she never really understood that we didn't want that from her and Dad. We preferred the gifts they made us. Mom and Dad were self-employed in a small-town catering business for more than forty years, and they had to be clever to support themselves and their family for so long. With the births of six kids spread over twenty years, there were plenty of opportunities for originality.

Jack made wonderful wooden gifts for his children and grandchildren. When the first three of us were preschool age, he built us wooden benches painted with our names on them: Jean, Tony, and Julie. The benches became our stepping stools to reach for things and start on our independence. When turned over and "hooked" together, the benches made an excellent train. We sat in them and took trips to the lake, to Minnesota to visit our grandparents, and anywhere that sounded fanciful. We were limited only by our imaginations. Fifty-two years later, my bench looks like it lived hard but survived. Dad also made benches for the next generation, and they were used in the same way.

In the Sixties, my tan playhouse with the white trim windows sat in a corner of the backyard. It was the only playhouse for blocks around and was a popular place to play. Every summer Dad added something new to the playhouse—a single white porch that covered the door, a bay window on the south side—and when he painted the main house blue with white trim, the playhouse, too, changed colors.

In order to keep the boys out of the playhouse, Dad built my brother Tony a fort ten feet off the ground. It was just a wooden platform, about four by four foot, mounted on unfinished tree poles with a ladder for entrance up the side. All the neighborhood kids played in our yard. It was the coolest place to be. The girls played dress-up in my playhouse, and the boys played cowboys and Indians in the fort.

It didn't stop when we got older. Everyone in my family has benefited from my parents' creative gift giving. There were snowmen fireplace screens, tables, hope chests, cradles, a fly-fishing chest, cute wooden shelves, and hanging plant gazebos. The grandchildren received forts, bags of blocks, and wooden boxes all handmade by Grandpa Jack. Recently, he made a birdhouse and a shield with his oldest great-grandson. The list is long.

My favorite gift is the dollhouse I received for Christmas when I was forty. A couple of years before, I had purchased a dollhouse kit because I was intrigued by miniatures. However, I could never find the time, space, or, mainly, motivation to work on it. My mother knew all of this, of course, because I told her everything during our daily chats. That August she found an old magazine from the fifties with a picture of a dollhouse, handed it to my Dad, and said, "Jack, make this for Jean for Christmas."

Dad said he made it because Mom had absolute faith he could, even though there were no instructions or measurements. So I finally got a dollhouse, and it is my prized possession. If, heaven forbid, my real house ever catches fire, I have figured out how to save the dollhouse. Everything else can burn.

Mom was also very crafty and made wonderful gifts for us. She made doll clothes when we were little and wreaths when we had homes. One item that she was famous for around town was her beautiful origami stars. When she was newly married in the mid-fifties, she found an article in *Good Housekeeping* magazine on how to make 3-D stars from four eleven-by-quarter-inch strips of paper. These were used on our Christmas tree every year so the tree would look good during the day with the lights turned off. She would give them as gifts, and during the lean years she would even sell them. She tried to teach me how to make them several times but, alas, I could never get the hang of it.

· We Came Back to Say ·

She would tell me, "You're just like your Grandpa Gaines. He always thought it was easy but couldn't get the hang of it either."

That's why I have saved several hundred of them. I have a plan to evacuate these along with the dollhouse.

❖

It wasn't called the Cookie Scholarship in the beginning. There was no name for it other than cookie cards.

Andrew was the first grandson to graduate from high school, in 2000. Jack and Wilma were stumped as to what to give him for a gift. Mom as usual wished she could buy him something meaningful.

I asked Mom, "What could you give to Andrew that he would like?"

"Food."

"What kind of food?"

"Cookies."

"Why don't you send him cookies every month?"

"That would be too often."

"Let me think about this for a few minutes to figure out how to make it a gift."

"That would be great!"

I thought of the logistics of this type of gift. Teenage boys need to be encouraged to write to their grandparents who don't have e-mail. So we started with that. It had to be short, because the boys couldn't focus on writing a whole letter. Postcard size was perfect. The cards had three choices of cookies listed with a check box next to each and then a space for writing. Andrew was to pick one type of cookie, write a note to Grandma and Grandpa about how he was doing, make sure his correct return address was there, and drop it in the mail. Leaving nothing to gum up the works, the cards were preaddressed and stamped. The cookies would arrive about ten days later.

When Andrew received this at his graduation party, he was thrilled and couldn't wait to use the cards. When he arrived at school that fall, his roommate loved it, too, and on one of the cards they asked for lasagna. Grandma sent it to them. It was a great way for her to keep in touch with her grandson and show her love. The buzz around the family was that it made Andrew very popular in his dorm.

Andrew was also happy to be the first, declaring, "I am the official taster for any new cookies that Grandma tries. So, far they have all been good and my new favorites, but I will keep trying."

The following year, Ryan was the second grandson to receive the cookie cards. Mom didn't know if this would be a popular gift until Ryan announced at his high school graduation, "Great! I got the Cookie Scholarship!"

The name stuck, and the rest of the grandsons looked forward hopefully to their turn.

Chad's favorite was Grandma's cinnamon rolls, so of course he received cards for fresh cinnamon rolls. Luckily he attended the University of Montana, where Grandma could just drive over to his apartment to deliver them.

Ben followed. He loved cookies but always said he didn't need any cards—Grandma would send him cookies whenever he asked. "Thanks, Grandma, but you know I'm just going to tell you when I need cookies regardless of how many cards I have. As the favorite grandson, I'm sure you'll send me cookies." He knew Grandma was a pushover and would always feed her grandsons. However, he did use his cards.

About this time the Cookie Scholarship took on a life of its own. When Wilma went to FedEx to send off a cookie box, the girls at the desk yelled, "The Cookie Lady is here! Where are they going today?"

They would tell her they were jealous of her grandsons, and occasionally Mom would bring a plate of cookies for the workers. She was very popular! She shipped the cookies to Tacoma and Spokane, Washington, and Durango and Fort Collins, Colorado.

Roommates of the grandsons asked if they could get their own scholarship. But this was only for Jack and Wilma's grandkids. As people heard of the Cookie Scholarship, many moms asked if Wilma could do this for their kids at college. She briefly considered selling Cookie Scholarships as graduation gifts but decided it would be too much work and would lose the specialness for the grandkids.

Cousin Chris followed Ben and was a little bit craftier than those who had gone before him. He made his cards last for all four years at college because he was smart enough to photocopy them. Chris has a flair for business. When Ryan, his older brother, found out, he protested, "No fair! You've broken the rules of the Cookie Scholarship."

· *We Came Back to Say* ·

We didn't know there were rules.

Joe followed his big brother Ben to college in Tacoma. Joe's favorite from Grandma was her chocolate sheet cake. So that was a choice on his cards in addition to cookies. He liked the cake so much he asked for the recipe from Grandma and started making his own cake after the cards were used. Joe shared with all of his friends.

Steven was the last to get the Cookie Scholarship while Mom was alive. At his graduation party, when he opened it he ran over to Grandpa and bowed down in front of him. "I've been waiting for the Cookie Scholarship for years!"

His roommates and dorm mates waited anxiously for the packages to arrive from Grandma and Grandpa.

Mom baked all the cookies, cakes, cinnamon rolls, and lasagna, while Dad came up with creative ways to ship the food so it arrived whole and delicious. Half the fun for the boys was tearing through the boxes to see what Grandpa had wrapped.

Mom passed away in 2007, shortly after sending a package of sweet buns to my friend Laure for her fiftieth birthday.

❖

There were two more graduations the summer of 2012. I felt sad that Mom wasn't around to do the Cookie Scholarship, and I shared this feeling with my siblings. Carol, my sister, asked if it would be all right if she did the Cookie Scholarship for our niece and nephew who were graduating.

"That would be fine, but you need to check with Dad to see if he's okay with that."

She called me back the next day. "He loves the idea!"

So once again I created the cards, and Carol now will bake and send the cookies.

Sam graduated in May. When he opened the Cookie Scholarship, we had to explain to him what it was as neither his brother Anthony nor his sister Sarah had received it. I explained how it worked and he thought it sounded pretty good. Anthony had just finished his first year at the University of Montana and said, "That's awesome!" I then realized that Anthony had not received the cookie gift because he didn't attend college until three years after he graduated from high school. I think he will receive it this fall.

· *Jean Engler* ·

Courtney graduated in June. She was aware of the Cookie Scholarship because her brothers had received it. She sadly said to her mom a few weeks before graduation, "I won't be able to get the Cookie Scholarship because Grandma's not here." Courtney was delighted to discover that the tradition carries on.

DEE'S LOFT

By Joyce Tomlinson

I MET DEE DURING A BRITTLE NEW YORK WINTER, both of us students of bookbinding at the Center for Book Arts. I noticed her on the first day, sitting alone at one of the waist-high worktables, and I sat down across from her. She looked to be in her fifties and didn't try to hide it—greying brown hair, no makeup. Her world-weariness intrigued me, maybe because in spite of it, her eyes lit up whenever she talked about Harvey.

Dee and Harvey were amateur photographers, and she'd signed up for bookbinding to learn how to turn their photos into coffee table books. I wanted the skills to bind my journals and essay collections with fabric and colored leather. Book Art was to be my gateway into the art world, a craft I thought even the talentless could learn. After thirty-plus years of marriage and child rearing, I needed an interest that was mine alone, and I'd left my husband at home in Seattle.

Dee and I shared tools and glue pots all week, struggling together to line up book board and shave leather for bindings. We ate pizza on our lunch breaks and poked around the nearby secondhand shops and book stores before heading back for afternoon classes. I learned that Dee and Harvey spent their winters at their loft in New York, summers at their farm upstate, and spring and fall at their flat in Paris. We talked about getting together after the class ended, to keep up our new friendship.

For the week of class I stayed with my daughter Katie and her husband Bill, who lived just eight blocks from the center. Katie and Bill collect photographs, so on the last day of class, Dee and I made a plan: first I'd take her to see their extensive collection, then we would go to her loft to admire Harvey's work. He had recently completed a series that she was excited to show me.

At the end of the day, we left the workshop and tramped through slush down Fifth Avenue toward Katie's place. The cold weather didn't seem to discourage New Yorkers—the sidewalks were as jam-packed as usual. The only difference from my last visit in the summer was that instead of sunglasses, the vendors were displaying wool scarves on their card tables.

When we finally reached Katie's building, we let ourselves in to her empty apartment and took off our coats and boots just inside the door.

"Well, here we are," I said. "Let's start in the living room."

Photographs were strategically hung throughout their home, some black and white, some color, all of them carefully selected with the help of an art broker.

"This is by Vic Muniz," I said, pointing out the portrait of Elvis drawn in chocolate syrup.

"I recognize it," Dee said. "And this is Cindy Sherman." She nodded toward a photograph of a pregnant woman dressed as Medusa, oatmeal-colored snakes sprouting from her head like squirming dreadlocks. "And Nick Cave."

"Right," I said. "You know your photographers."

"Some people only buy art as an investment," she sniffed. "Most times it doesn't matter to them if they even like it—it's all about the money they can make. There's no connection."

"Oh I don't know," I said. "I think Katie and Bill like all the work they have on their walls. Besides, if it weren't for collectors, how would artists make a living?"

"Well, someday they'll be collecting Harvey's work," she said. "He's an artiste."

After a cursory glance at the rest of the photos, she reached for her belongings. I began to wonder whether she was at all interested in any photography but Harvey's. Maybe she would feel the same about any passion of his.

We flagged a taxi and watched it cut across two lanes of traffic, splashing through puddles as it went, landing a few feet from the curb in front of us. We climbed in, still talking.

· We Came Back to Say ·

"Just wait until you see Harvey's work," Dee said. As we cruised across town, she told me how Harvey had made his fortune developing digital color printing for computers. The two of them met years ago in California, where they worked at the same university. Both had children from previous marriages. He was the love of her life, she said. A genius. Forward-thinking. A Renaissance man, not bound by society's conventions. While she talked I just kept thinking, Jeez, I hope his work is decent.

The cab pulled up to a stately prewar building. "This is it," she said.

I paid the driver and we stepped out of the cold into a simple lobby, no doorman. Dee was uncharacteristically quiet on the ride up to her floor, but as the elevator opened I could swear she winked at me.

We pushed open the heavy doors to the apartment. There, on every wall, were larger-than-life photographs of a young woman, stark naked. In some of the pictures she was laughing, her long, red hair falling across her face. In others she grimaced, hands clenched into fists.

Her thin, boyish body was covered in freckles, making her look twelve years old, and in every picture seventy-something Harvey Sullivan had his face planted firmly in her crotch.

The pictures focused tightly on the two of them, with no background except a white sheet. The scene was repeated over and over on every inch of space on every wall.

I took a breath, trying to focus on the sliver of brick wall between the pictures, or the one piece of furniture I could see, a bed in the middle of the room. Fight-or-flight adrenaline rushed through my body and I quickly went over the last hour in my mind, trying to remember any comment of Dee's that might have prepared me for this. All I could think of was "not bound by society's conventions." You could say that again.

Harvey emerged from a walled-off part of the loft and I heard Dee say, "Harvey, this is Joyce. Joyce, Harvey."

"Hello," I said. "I've been hearing about you." I didn't offer my hand.

Dee and Harvey watched my face, poised expectantly with their eyes gleaming, for my reaction. They exchanged a glance that said, *this is going to be good*, and it dawned on me that shocking people was the whole point of this.

Suddenly the last thing I wanted to do was give them the satisfaction of seeing me freak out. The unflappable part of my brain took control. I would remain calm, at least for the time it took to tour the "artiste's" work and get the hell out. Let someone else get them off.

I leaned forward, looking closely at the photograph in front of me and fixating on the redheaded girl's feet. They were filthy.

"You couldn't take this girl for a pedicure?" I said.

"Oh, no. No," Harvey said. "This is reality. These are real people."

Ah, I nodded. Real. A white-haired old dude going down on a girl young enough to be his granddaughter.

"Who is she?" I said.

"Oh, she lives in the neighborhood. Artists' model," Harvey said.

"You paid her to do the series?"

"Sure," Harvey said. "Bought her lunch, gave her a few bucks."

Again I nodded. A faint throbbing began in my temples.

I looked at Dee. "Why aren't you in these pictures?"

"Because I'm not twenty-four years old," Dee said. "No one wants to see this." She looked down at her lumpy body, smoothed back her greying hair.

But it would be real, I thought.

Harvey was covered in all the pictures—he'd hidden his lumpy body with a stained bathrobe and white crew sox. The bottoms of his stockings showed the grimy outline of all his toes, the shape of his foot. In person he wore black-rimmed glasses, but in the photographs he was evidently feeling his way. His face was hidden in most of the pictures, but in one or two—when he was coming up for air—you could see his flabby profile against a background of red pubic hair.

I examined each picture, nodding my head and saying "nice colors," and "interesting lighting." Disgusting as this setup was, it was also oddly fascinating. I was walking with this guy's wife through his sexual fantasy—which didn't include her—and she was smiling.

Harvey showed me his cameras and the lighting equipment he'd rigged up so he could star in his own photos. He explained the color processing system he'd developed that made them so intensely vivid, while the redheaded girl's eyes looked down at us from every wall.

We sat down at the table so they could show me Harvey's portfolios. I opened the first one and flipped through. Page after page were photographs of clothing arranged in sexual poses. Men's shirts and pants giving oral sex to women's clothes. There were no people in the pictures, just different brightly colored outfits.

Some of the clothes from Harvey's portfolio hung in the open closet across from where I was sitting. He said they were his ex-wife's things, a blue flowered silk kimono, bright green blouse, pink dress. And there was the white bathrobe, hanging on a hook next to them.

I tried to imagine what it was like to be Dee, living there, looking at this stuff day and night. What was the message Harvey was sending with these pictures? Was it 'look what I can do?' Did he want his wife—and the rest of the world—to see him satisfying someone else, someone young? I wondered where Dee had been when the redheaded girl was in the loft being photographed with Harvey, if the two women met, became friends. Dee seemed to go along with Harvey's obsession, but maybe she thought she didn't have a choice.

Dee and I rode down together in the elevator and made small talk. I asked her how long they would be in the city, what was next for her. Stepping outside I pulled my coat tight around me and said goodbye, knowing I would never see her again. As I turned to walk away, Dee put her hand on my shoulder to stop me and smiled right up close to my face, confidential-like.

"That's my bad boy," she said.

SOMETHING CLICKS INTO PLACE

By Carmen D'Arcangelo

I NOTICE HIS WEDDING BAND on the speckled granite countertop. Behind it perch glass jars of half empty Aztec grains and an aquamarine collecting tray tumbling over with old keys, assorted fi-it tools and pieces of a tiny plastic pig game.

I pretend I am a stranger to this house, which in some ways I am. What story could I tell?

…A sizeable wedding band—could it be briefly abandoned so the owner can lay capable hands on a table saw, a brake pad, or a lover's body?

…Old keys—could the family have recently moved, still stumbling amidst the tsunami wave of old habits meeting new entryways?

…Assorted tools—do they live in the physical world of installing, constructing, rebuilding with tangible materials-wood, wires and widgets? *I imagine them moving beyond the physical world to repair intangible breakages.*

…Plastic pig game—a rowdy adventuresome gang, plastic pigs and giggling children rolling dice during tiny moments of physical rest

But I am not a stranger and I know this story. Tonight he sleeps in the garage on a futon. The 'Soaring Heart Natural Bedding' Futon I slept on with the baby for fifteen sleepless months. The baby he acquiesced to having.

"I was already at capacity with two children. I feel like I was set up to fail."

· *We Came Back to Say* ·

I cock my eyebrows when this statement arrives at regular intervals. How many people does it take to make a baby?

I wonder how much of our cumulative marriage we have each slept alone on that futon. My dazzling, silver haired, entertain-the-masses mother-in-law claimed that she had only spent 4 years together with her first husband of twenty-one years. Is that a good thing I wonder? "Absence makes the heart grow fonder," *they* say. Do I believe that?

Does it matter? Separation is hard for me—the only child raised by a grandmother in a foreign country for the first eight years. I met my mother sometime during 3rd grade after moving across the Atlantic and stumbling through learning English by watching endless episodes of *I Dream of Jeannie*. I still remember the morning she rises early and boils me the perfect egg. While sitting at our 50s era dinette set she looks across at me, deeply dragging from her Marlboro Light. Something inside me clicks into place and I know she is expecting to assume her role as mother. I let her.

And spend my life separated from my grandmother. Separation of spirit. Separation of space. It follows me like a persistent guest unwilling to depart.

Recently my family of three children and one husband moved from the 1907 farm house we lovingly restored (our first baby-no futon yet). We bundled and brought all three subsequent children home to its warm embrace. Eleven years of nursing, hammering, and birthday celebrations around the corner pine kitchen nook with the little dings and paint marks, testament to years of creation.

I remember the early years where I had to remind him to let me change a diaper; actively participating, proactive, a drunk-with-baby-love Dad. *This is so easy, so much fun; let's do it again.* Fifteen months later we had child number two. No one slept for a year, he pulled away, spending more and more time in (guess where) the garage – and I paddled my family lifeboat. I rolled up my mother sleeves, put my head down and gnashed my way through the early years of two children under two, under three, under four. When I looked up he was gone. Not physically. He still carted truckloads of topsoil, took the children swimming, and persevered in his ever-changing merchant marine schedule. But he had taken himself, or I had pushed him, out of the sphere of relevance and inclusion in the family. I was alone in lifeboat; isolated and hungry for attention, groping in the dark.

· *Carmen D'Arcangelo* ·

Over the next years I collected male attention like colorful beach glass trinkets. There was a young, sweet-eyed, rebellious barista, an emotional-intelligence consultant and recovering SA (I learned that meant sex addict), a crazy, curly haired Russian-Jewish soul level astrologer, and finally even a vintage-era boyfriend reinserted himself. All tempting and all ultimately kept in my fantasy world. I squeezed his hand and breathlessly committed all those years ago. *I do* sticks with the hard times.

So we start to read books;

The Good Marriage

The Passionate Marriage

Too Good to Leave, Too Bad to Stay

Sex and the Seasoned Woman

The last book we had read together was *Snow falling on Cedars* during our honeymoon when life and love was easy. The searing rocks and glistening beaches of the Greek islands too small to cradle our love back then – 13 years ago. The open bodied sex and ease of every day. Life can grind this kind of love. "It is not meant to stay," *they* say. I disagree. I want that back. I'm forty-three not one hundred and three.

We attend marital counseling, sitting in faux leather chairs commenting on the interesting choices of art on the walls. Can he forgive me? Can he accept his role as a father of three? Can I let him back in? Can I accept his need for time alone?

Now in bits and shreds we are leaving behind the previous era; the young love; the house; the child making; the separations. I'm suddenly a small child again sitting across the table from my mother. Something clicks. I need to leave the separation behind so we can reattach.

I don't yet understand how to do this.

I don't yet understand marriage thirteen years in. Does anybody?

A TASTE OF HOME
By Amber Wong

My apron's on and I'm at the stove cooking *bok chik gai*, Chinese steamed chicken in ginger and scallion sauce, Alex's favorite dish. I hear an unfamiliar rumble in the driveway and peek out the window. I rush to the sink, dunk my greasy hands in warm, soapy water, and quickly swipe them, palms first, then backs, on my apron. I'm at the front door in two seconds. I throw it open and struggle to keep myself from racing out like a madwoman.

The U-Haul truck has just pulled up and my 19-year-old son Alex, tall and slender like his father, jumps out of the driver's seat with an easy grin and a bright "Hey Mom!" He turns to the truck and I see him glance down to make sure he has the keys in hand before he reaches in to lock the door. He doesn't need to lock it; the truck is empty. But he does it out of habit, and I know he'd say I taught him that. He turns toward me, and with the sun luminously backlighting his reddish hair and the glint of the September sun off Lake Washington, he looks like an angel. He doesn't know it, but he's breaking my heart.

Today Alex is heading back to college in San Diego. He's already spent his freshman year in the dorm, coming home to Seattle only for Christmas and Easter, so I should be used to his absence. For a whole year, he rarely called or wrote. Even though I'd steeled myself for his initial surge into independence, I hadn't expected his virtual disappearance from my life. My friends heard from their kids at least every week, some heard up to three times a day—a call, a text message, just saying hi or asking for advice. I felt left out, abandoned by a child who had always been a good communicator. In a vacuum, I worried, *is he okay?* I grew suspicious: *is he still attending class?* After two weeks of no news, I'd send him a friendly email, follow up with a voicemail, and finally culminate in an urgent text: *"Alive?"* with the mutual understanding that if I didn't hear back within an hour I'd call the cops. Even an unembellished *"Yes"* would suddenly turn my two weeks of annoyance into a day of joy.

So after a whole summer of seeing him every day, why is my heart racing, why am I on the verge of tears? Why am I resisting this leave-taking, a transition that is natural, normal, the best thing in the world for him? After all, it was me who insisted that he go away to college to experience a different part of the country, meet new people, learn to rely on himself. But now, against all of my better instincts, I find myself wanting to draw him back. Perhaps I'd thought of San Diego as a grand adventure, a short trip to the beach, a flight with a return ticket. Up until now, I naively assumed he'd come back—Seattle is his home. But today, seeing him standing next to the U-Haul truck, it hits me: he's *moving*. He's taking his bed, our old couch, and all of his belongings to his new apartment. He's making a home in San Diego. Once that's done, it will take more than hope, or serendipity, to bring Alex back into my orbit.

I know this because I'm the daughter who never came home. After college, I left California for a job in Washington, and, 34 years later, I'm still here. The first two years, my parents didn't question my choice—it was my first job, after all, and I was getting valuable experience. But as time went on and I took a new job, and then another, they, along with my aunts and uncles, started asking more pointedly, *so, when are you coming home?* as if it were always a given that I'd be back. I'd be caught short trying to explain that I had no plans to move back to California. They grew more insistent when I married and had two sons; after all, grandsons (and, by extension, great-nephews) should be doted upon. But after I survived a divorce when my sons were barely in elementary school without going home, the comments faded away. Was I just branded a renegade, the one who never returned? Or did I break my parents' hearts, too?

Alex strides into the house and casually drapes his arm over my shoulders. His eyes are bright, excited. "See Mom, the van can hold everything I need for my apartment!" He squeezes my shoulder and then releases me, heading toward the stairwell. As he clomps down to the basement on his size-12 feet, he calls over his shoulder, "I'll start bringing up the boxes now, and then we can pack everything in!" It's a given that I'll help him with this task. His voice fades as he turns the corner and eases into his room.

His room. I catch myself. Is it really even *his* room? Since we moved to a new house this summer, he has inhabited a room that I originally thought of as "the guest room." Is he a guest now, or, as a fledgling adult, is he entitled to his own room here?

Alex and I talked about it that June night after I picked him up at the airport at the end of his freshman year. He was excited to be home for the summer. But "home" was then in transition—my new husband and I had just signed the papers to buy a house together, one that was big enough for our blended families to celebrate holidays together. We'd be moving the following month. So that night, I'd brought Alex back to *our* family home, the home he grew up in, the 1940s' rambler with the drum kit-and-guitar-appointed basement and huge maple-and-fir-studded yard, perfect for raising young sons. It was natural for him to head straight down the hall to his dark-green bedroom, drop the four large duffel bags containing all his college possessions in a heap, and collapse onto his neatly made, freshly laundered bed. He rolled from side to side as he emptied his pockets on the nightstand. Then he reached for one of his pillows and scrunched it under his chin as he rolled onto his stomach to talk to me. In one moment, the room that for nine months had doubled as my office took on a distinct air of maleness, sweat, and dishevelment.

I sat in the desk chair, swiveled around to see him. His long legs hung over the edge, his 6'2" frame too large for even a double bed.

"We're moving," I ventured, watching for his reaction. "We signed the papers last week. It's done."

He looked around the room, *his* room. Posters of two girls in shorts—generic, smiling faces, curvy rear ends—were still tacked to the walls we'd painted together. The brown rug with his stylized initials in the middle, originally custom-made for my father, but now his, covered the hardwood floor. Above his dresser hung the picture I took long ago of him with his arm around Sarah, two smiling three-year-olds, best buddies and next-door neighbors, both unaware that in the next hour she'd be moving far away to Colorado. This room held eighteen years of him.

Through the open door to his closet, I saw two stacks of repurposed blue, plastic baby-wipe boxes, the treasure boxes of his childhood. I smiled and shook my head at the early memory of myself, an earnest mom intent on teaching her son to put away his toys, with the added message of "Re-use what you have!" I'd labeled these boxes in clear, easy-to-read block writing—Alex's Matchbox Cars, Alex's Knight Box, Alex's Football Cards. Even though he was only four years old and couldn't yet read, it actually worked; he always put these toys away in the right boxes. Initially, I assumed that he simply memorized the letter patterns on the boxes. I was stunned when he went one step further: instead of randomly tossing all of his football cards back into the box, he actually kept them filed away by team.

This filing system was not my idea; it was my mother's. She was so focused on organizing us—from my kitchen drawers to the kids' bookshelves—that on her annual trip to Seattle, she stayed home by herself while I dropped the kids at day care and went to work. Using construction paper and tape, she labored an entire day making little colored envelopes with tabs on top: first the alphabet tabs, A to Z, and then the team tabs. She wrote the name of a football team on each tab—Denver Broncos, Oakland Raiders, San Francisco Forty-Niners, and all the rest—placed each envelope behind the proper alphabet tab, and put the whole thing in one of those blue baby-wipe boxes. I thought he'd never keep it organized, but I was wrong; Alex loved it. I'd peek in his room and see him poring over his cards. Ask him about a particular player, and he could easily find the card. When he'd get a new pack of football cards, he'd rip it open and within five minutes he'd have all the new players correctly filed away with their teams.

I heard the bed creak as Alex rocked over on one hip and continued to consider his room: Beanie Babies on his dresser, two little handmade pillows from Aki Kurose, his first-grade teacher, at the head of his bed. He caught me glancing at from the closet; I raised an eyebrow and smiled at him. He automatically turned to the closet, saw the boxes, and gave me a knowing grin. Of course, he knew what I was thinking; it had always been this way. Starting before he could walk, we had that sixth sense about each other. Even his day-care teachers noticed; they told me that he'd suddenly stop playing and look toward the door, and invariably I would just be arriving to see him.

· We Came Back to Say ·

His eyes wandered back to those little pillows, and his smile of recognition would have warmed Aki's heart. The mementoes were significant: a red-and-white-print heart to signify world peace, a luminous square cream plush to remind him of the phases of the moon. These were two of Aki's biggest lessons. Aki's first grade class would sing the peace song, in different languages, every morning, followed by identifying the phase of the moon that night – a waxing gibbous? A waning crescent? Those memories, tucked deep into his subconscious, surfaced briefly; we shared them for a moment before they submerged again. He turned to me.

"It's okay, Mom," he said finally, "I don't live here anymore. Whatever you want to do is okay. If you want to move, that's fine with me."

There was something halting in his tone—or did I just imagine it? He was being gracious, kind, but somehow the simple statement "I don't live here anymore" was like a dissonant chord. I didn't want to hear it.

His tone was so different from a mere three months ago, as was mine. When he was home in March for the week of spring break, he was sarcastic, absent, preoccupied. I felt like kicking him out right then. He had a girlfriend in Seattle and was gone most of the week. She'd call and he'd leap up, announce he had to go, and not come home until three in the morning.

I confronted him one afternoon in the kitchen as he stood in his flannel pajama pants, hair mussed, chest bare, face illuminated by the light from the open refrigerator. His eyes darted from shelf to shelf as he reached in to move some cartons aside. Without warning, I started in.

"Can't you get home by *one*?" I snapped. "You're being selfish and inconsiderate! You wake us all up when you come home!" The truth is, I'd be awake all night until I heard his key in the door.

"What? What the…" He straightened up and turned to face me, his lanky frame towering over mine. Suddenly, his eyes were on fire.

"You just want to control me! But I'm nineteen—I don't need to listen to you anymore!" He slammed the fridge shut and stood there, glaring.

Where had *that* come from? I wanted to yell, *Yeah, right—who's paying your tuition!* but managed to choke it back in time; I didn't want this argument to escalate to where he'd quit college just to make a point. Instead, I felt crushed by his rebelliousness, and by the depth of my feeling.

"You're not growing up to be the man that I thought you'd be!" I sputtered, angry tears threatening to blur my eyes. His eyes opened wide and I could see his jaw tense.

"I'm outta here!" he yelled, as he turned and left. It was painful; my son had turned into someone I didn't recognize. After that hellish week, I was dreading the summer.

So as I sat with him in his room, I marveled that he had returned as a more charming version of his original self. The last three months had transformed him in ways that I could never fully know. Another quarter had elapsed; was he newly proud that he'd found his academic focus? I had heard, indirectly, that he had broken up with his girlfriend—was he feeling more in control of his life? Perhaps he'd realized, as I had, that our balance of power was changing, that we should find a way to communicate on a more equal level. From personal experience, I knew that if I wanted to have a close relationship with my son, I had to change. My mother had not, and I was resolved not to repeat her mistake.

When we moved into the new house in July, I showed him the daylight basement bedroom where he would stay. He glanced around appreciatively.

"I got the worst bedroom in the house, and it's still great!" There was nothing snide or insincere about his comment. Even though he had no choice, he seemed happy, grateful just to have a place to stay.

So he spent the summer in that room, the new room he liked, and worked virtually full-time as a restaurant server. He'd wake up around noon and be home for a few hours before going back to work. When he had an early shift, he'd work from noon to nine. I didn't see him much. Although we only shared a few meals together and rarely shared an entire day, we were good. He was relaxed, chatty, and happy to be home.

Isn't this what I was striving for? A happy, healthy, independent child? I should be elated: the bulk of my parenting work done. My son has grown into a person I really like, someone I trust, someone with whom I can freely discuss issues or even make jokes. Someone who has qualities I admire in my best friends. Someone who holds my memories. Someone who understands me implicitly.

So why do I feel this way? Because I look into his eyes and know that he is like me. He will be gone, suddenly gone, off on his own journey. I feel that pang again.

Alex bounds back up the stairs, carrying a box full of dishes. This is the set of twenty-four dinner plates that my mother gave me so many years ago. *Banquet china*, she said, as if everyone should have some. She could never resist a bargain: fifty cents a plate at Safeway if you bought fifty dollars' worth of groceries. The ultimate hostess, she said that all you needed were the dinner plates when you entertained. She had a set, I had a set, my brother had a set—all sets of twenty-four, just in case we broke a couple. We were expected to carry on that tradition of inviting people to our homes, cooking for large crowds, and we did. That fortune in groceries formed my taste of home, with the plates as souvenirs. Not that he knows, or needs to know, that history.

"Thanks, Mom, these will be great!" he exults. He strides into the kitchen to seal the box with packing tape.

Another box emerges, then another. The "Blue Cornflower" CorningWare that my mother carefully packed in old dishtowels for me when I got my first job and moved a thousand miles away. The pots, pans, and cookie sheets—remnants of the wedding gifts from my marriage to Alex's father—carefully culled from my kitchen. The cooking utensils that I've used to make him endless meals of spaghetti, stir-fry chicken, garlic prawns, *bok chik gai*, rice. Everything tinged with familiar flavors, all the makings of home. I've packed all these boxes and left them, unsealed, downstairs. He glances at them, oblivious to the hours of sifting, the care wrapped tight around each piece. It's good he doesn't know. It's just too much to know.

After our feast of chicken and rice, I give him one last hug and send him on his way. Tears well as I softly close the door and hear the truck begin its slow rumble down the street. He can't see me, but he knows, because two days later he cheers me with a surprise check-in call: "Just arrived in San Diego, Mom, all safe and sound." He sounds happy, so I am, too.

It's a jagged dance, but I must come to terms with not knowing the full details of his life, must learn to view him with some emotional distance. But finding that sweet spot—far enough to let him grow, close enough for him to feel connected—is a skill so hard to master. It's a fragile balance, so much at stake.

END OF THE LINE
By Linda Zbigley

Waiting for a train is like death sitting with Ron.

Nowhere to go.

In the right place.

Waiting for the train and riding it home in the middle of the night,

Exhaustion rattles my sleep in wakefulness.

I peek out the window from time to time to see where we are. Is there anything I recognize?

Riding the train at night, I expect to see something I know.

Waiting in death

There is nothing to recognize.

Stopping.

Trains stop.

Rides are interrupted

With Ron moving towards death,

Death is a smooth mesmeric lull.

Sitting parallel to the one I love.

· *We Came Back to Say* ·

Still carrying a little sadness for Ron in my left jowl and eye, a bit of muscle locks as water begins to drip from the right corner of my eye, nearly eight summers after his passing. As time passes I sometimes reflect on my memories of Ron, and I think, "What more can we ask than the pleasure of each other's company?" In my desire to stay with my dear Ron as the pain of esophageal cancer became real enough to make him see a doctor, I have learned not to fear aging and death so much.

Why was I there? That's simple. I loved being with him. I wasn't there because he was sick. Yes, I did some care-giving, but that's not why I was with him. That kind of "Let me take care of you; I'll solve all your problems" behavior that I knew so well in myself earlier in life wasn't prevalent in my relationship with this man. I was with Ron because he had so much life in him.

Ron was a good man. He made me laugh. Ron, the well-shouldered blond I wished had asked me to the high school prom. Ron, whom I next met at our 30th class reunion, where we talked animatedly for an hour. Ron, whom I emailed through Classmates.com seven years later, who noticed and responded to me this time. We began to date, ever so slowly getting acquainted. Ron had been married and divorced twice. His second wife had blown his pension with schemes that never panned out. No third strikes for him. Ron was not interested in marriage to me. Yet we had a great time together.

In August 2001, thirty-seven years after high school, we began to connect. We emailed for months, and then talked on the phone for more. Becoming friends, we met for walks, followed by a few hikes in the Cascades and later a favorite walk of Ron's up to the Nisqually Glacier on Mt. Rainier. Then came a very different kind of date. We both knew it.

Whenever we made a transition in relationship, in that instance Ron would say, "Let's see, how are we going to do this?" Of course, we never defined the word "this." We only decided where to meet which that afternoon would be Lincoln Park in West Seattle.

As our friendship began I had only worn pants, but this date would be different and I had to prepare. I was beginning to feel more feminine around him. Ron's sturdy, masculine physique and general manliness was bringing out my feminine. I needed to find a dress. My wardrobe was lacking in that department. So, it was time to go shopping.

When that afternoon arrived, putting on my new Asian-styled aqua blue dress increased my sense of womanliness. I felt great. I had fun getting ready. I was taking on the full role. Neither of us said so, yet we both knew this would be our first date to dress up.

I drove over to the park early. For me to have been on time would have shown that this was obviously a special date; early was remarkable. Ron drove in after work, arriving his usual few minutes early. Tonight, I thought, I intended to be seductive. Taking that in, I felt playful waiting for him. After all, wasn't I wearing my favorite black lingerie and that new dress, just for him? As Ron drove into the parking lot, I stood with a pinwheel in my hand, making sure he could see me as he parked. I walked up to him in the driver's seat and stood flirting with a pinwheel as if I were a teen BUtterfield 8 with a lollipop. The ruse started out fine, but then I felt sheepish *trying* to be sexy. Embarrassed, I nearly stopped, jumping back into my usual unisex earthy style. But there I was standing with this whirling thing in my hand.

"Hi Ron," I said, trying to hide behind the pinwheel.

Looking at me, he smiled lightly, "Hi Linda."

As our relationship progressed, I found that most of the time, Ron couldn't touch me, and he didn't like being touched. Once, early on, while riding in the car, I stroked his neck. After about ten minutes, he asked me, "Please stop. Touching the back of my neck gives me the creeps." I recoiled, pulling my hand back, nearly jumping back to the window. I was shocked. I don't like to bring discomfort to anyone. But we were becoming closer in so many ways, and I take great pleasure in touch, especially touching someone like Ron who I cared about. I was confused, and I was left with my emotions and desire to touch and be touched stuck in the back of my throat.

I never figured this out. After Ron's death I returned love letters to his college sweetheart. When I to talked her about Ron's hating to be touched, she was really surprised. In his college years, just after Vietnam, Ron was most sensuous and pleasing. She said this Ron who could hardly tolerate being touched was not the Ron she knew. After a hell of a few Vietnam years, walking point, sitting in the DMZ, PTSD had to kick in sometime, somehow. I think Ron's PTSD expressed itself in his getting the creeps, goose bumps, and his hair standing on end from the touch of another person. Who knows? Maybe it got worse when he gave up drinking fifteen years before I met him.

So, in bed I didn't snuggle up close to him, making sure not to touch at all. Instead, I waited for him to initiate touch. Later, in his own time, he would move over making love to me when I was drowsy. Ron would snuggle his nose into my ear, tickling and delighting my senses. I felt like he was a puppy dog and I would giggle. Ron would explore pleasing me, but I still was awkward in touching him. Darned if I could figure him out.

Over the five years of slowly getting acquainted, we came to love each other. Of course, there was so much more to know, mysteries to uncover. I expected we would have decades to enjoy together. My family is long-lived. Ron's is not. While I knew Ron, one family member died of cancer each year. I was sorry for his grief, never guessing he would be next.

Then, suddenly, it was Ron dying of cancer. Ron may have been suspicious of his own illness much earlier, but he never mentioned it. He only spoke of cancer and death in his family. In his manly way, Ron never had any more to do with physicians than the required annual medical exams for work. Ron was beyond surviving cancer before he looked into his health insurance policy and made a first appointment. Ron began talking about illness only a little earlier, but it was only acid reflux, which for him baking soda satisfied.

It seemed as though we had hardly begun to know each other when he had received his diagnosis of metastatic esophageal cancer. I don't remember being mad then, but I am now. At that time my only concern was for him. I've gone through a period of blaming Ron for his own demise. He never maintained regular check-ups with a general practitioner, not even through his decades of acid reflux following Vietnam. Instead, Ron waited until his cancer had metastasized before getting a medical workup. He avoided doctors like my grandparents from the Old Country did, using home remedies instead of visiting clinics. He took himself away from me, is the way I felt.

Being a school teacher, once school was out in June I was glad I would have more time with Ron, more than the usual weekend sleepovers when I was working. During his last four days I remained with

Ron, visiting a little, helping when I could. Before Ron died, he asked if there was anything I'd like.

"What about your Rainier Beach High School letterman's jacket?" I answered. Ron lettered in football and baseball. Couldn't help asking for that jacket, even though I knew it was going to his grandson. Ron had handed it to me to try on a year earlier. I wouldn't call him a jock, but he didn't fall into the category of nerd like many guys in my honors classes. Ron dated in high school; I didn't. Now meeting him in our fifties I would ask him about what I missed in high school. There were only a few things like slow-dancing bodies moving close together I wanted. And he'd oblige, even though that was about the only kind of dancing he could do. That and just moving loosely, freely, wildly, and with fun to the music. I enjoyed dancing like that, too, but I wanted to know what slow dancing was like with someone I loved.

A little more clarification of what I couldn't have: "Well, you can have almost anything. The grandfather clock goes to Tara, "Ron continued, declaring his daughter would get the clock. Good, because I wanted the softness of one of his pressed shirts. His fragrance infused into the fabric. I wanted something of him to touch and smell.

By the time Ron was given a diagnosis, cancer had spread throughout his body. At the end back pain forced him to buy a comfy, plush chair. And there he sat down. This was now Ron, Ron who almost never sat in recliners until a few months earlier. He called that chair his old man's chair and he rarely moved out of it. I was sad to see Ron changing so quickly, losing the strength and vitality he prided himself in.

In the spring of his last year, Ron stayed in his chair, watching. All day he sat, not moving much, watching as each of us entered, and visited. Watching from one place. During the chair period, I was often the only person there. Sometimes I wondered why, although I knew he had cherished his solitude outside work as much as I.

Unlike in my family, where most people live past eighty and with quite a few still around at ninety, many in Ron's family were already dead. One after another relative had died of cancer. Many more would follow soon after him. Work and time had distanced his friends.

Ron's stepdaughter, Tara, stayed at Ron's the last couple of days he lived. But she rarely came into his bedroom. She couldn't stand the blood, that coffee-grounds-colored blood that came from his insides.

· We Came Back to Say ·

Ron's mother dropped by his home occasionally, as well. He was her favorite son. She stayed longer the last couple of days of his life, but she hardly left a large soft guest chair in his basement rec room. At the time I didn't understand why the stairs were so difficult for her to climb. She died of brain cancer two years later. Death surrounded and cradled this family, leaving only his sister LaDonna alive shortly after that.

So, what did I want to remember Ron by? A strange thing to ask while he was alive and in front of me. And yet, that day, I would choose something to take home with me. "Ron, give me one of your shirts."

Without a comment or a second's thought, Ron looked toward the hallway, directing me. I got up and turned away from him as he sat surrounded by chair. Slowly I moved down the hallway, past the other rooms in his tri-level suburban seventies house toward the master bedroom. I never looked back, but I knew Ron was watching me in silence. Then, I turned out of sight.

Walking up to his closet, I rolled one of the two long sliding wood doors, until it stopped at the far side of the room. Revealed inside was a long line of neatly placed shirts. This was a collection of his working shirts. Presented before me was every kind of shirt from dress to casual, even old button-down collars, a full closet display like I'd never seen before, each shirt neatly ironed. I knew they were there, but had never paid such close attention to all of them together. In contrast, my clothes, shirts, skirts, pants, and dresses all fit into a space a quarter of this closet's length. His row of wall-to-wall shirts no longer shocked me as it once had. Time had changed that. Instead, Ron's shirts drew me in.

Abruptly, I stopped in place, overwhelmed by Ron's imminent death. I could smell him here, in his shirts. I found him there, vibrant in his shirts. Lifting my nose higher with a long, full suck of air, I took in this scent.

After a few minutes, I reached out and touched one, then another. I stroked their soft, smooth, ironed fabric. Next, I moved in closer, wiggling my shoulders to get in closer to him, the shirts almost surrounding me. My nose nestled in many shirt shoulders. I could linger here. But I could not choose. I only wanted him.

· *Linda Zbigley* ·

I suddenly popped awake by Ron's hoot down the hall, "Did you get lost in there?"

"No."

"OK," he said. I heard movement. He was up from his chair. Slowly, Ron walked up the hall, grunting a little. I backed out of the closet as he walked in. Going over to one of his dressers, he pulled on a drawer. Ron lifted out one sweater, then another, saying, "Maybe you'd like a sweater. My family gives me so many as Christmas presents. Here, you look good in blue." Then pointing across the room at another dresser he told me, "Over there are more to choose from." I looked down at the sweater Ron held up to me. I began to move. Somehow, it was easier for me to receive his sweaters and shirts with him in that space, in his bedroom, saying, "Here, take this one."

Ron died three weeks later. I found peace being together with Ron in the comfort of death. No fear. No forward. No backward. Just present. In the right place. And nowhere to go. We were comforted by death, centered in its sacredness, sacredness I could only call "truth" at that moment.

Yet after those pure days of being present with Ron, comforting death transforming him to the other side, I was exhausted. My exhaustion turned into action to prepare for his funeral. Time was expanded, filled full with emotions pushing my margins out. Sometimes I was stunned in that unusual territory death brings. Anger, nearly rage at his family's Lutheran minister during Ron's funeral blew up inside me. The liturgy of the funeral service was probably identical to what it had been fifty years ago. The minister would not allow others to speak or give eulogies during his service. Only after he finished the service and walked out, could friends and family approach the pulpit to say a few words in memory of Ron. I was angry at the minister for his hardness. It was easier to vent my anger at a living person. I could not imagine getting angry at my love now dead. Mostly, I was angry that Ron was dead.

Rage and anger didn't last long. A sense of Ron's sacred death was followed by wanting to go with him, unconsciously tumbling into the cascade, over the rocks of grief and into depression, depression speeding up my aging, until a velum of sleep surrounded me.

For some time after his death the words "Ron is gone. And he ain't never coming back" stood out loudly in my mind. I resided in that state of complex and shifting emotions, emotions that usually remain quiet and out of sight.

What is left after Ron is gone? Once again to fight my way out of drowsiness, by any means necessary, to focus again in life. Today, twelve years later, I know expressing my own anger wakes me. Exercise movement wakes me. Yet I must fight my own inertia to move. And sometimes I do.

After all, Ron didn't call me into death. He wanted me on earth, feet planted firmly, going forward. Didn't he give me this sweater of warmth? His handing me a sweater was like saying, "Goodbye now. I must go. But here, take one of my sweaters to wear as you go into the future. May it warm you. May your eyes shine blue wearing it."

CONTRIBUTORS

Faren Bachelis is a writer, editor, and photographer. She is the author of three books, including *The Pelican Guide to Sacramento and the Gold Country*. Her writing has appeared in newspapers and magazines including the *Seattle Times*, the *Sacramento Bee*, the *St. Louis Post-Dispatch*, and *Spindrift: Art and Literary Journal*. ImperfectBuddhist.com.

Christiane Banta was a 2007 Macy's Most Inspiring Breast Cancer Survivor essay contest winner and was a memoir finalist in the 2008 PNWA Literary Contest. She has a certificate in Popular Fiction from UW Professional and Continuing Education where she also studied memoir writing. She lives in Seattle with her partner, Jim.

Sandy Barnes has completed the Memoir Certificate program at the University of Washington. Her work has been featured in *Stratus: Journal of Arts & Writing*, Magic Cat Press, outwardlink.net and Milk Sugar. She lives near Seattle, Washington and is a late bloomer.

Johna Beall, MA is an author, psychologist, and business woman. A graduate of UC Berkeley at a historic time in the late 60s, her first publications were as editor of an underground newspaper. She has a great appreciation for friends, family, dogs; she's a student of music, mysticism, and sailing.

Paul Boardman lives in Seattle. By day he writes and at night works as a bartender, his second career after over twenty years in international trade. He grew up in Japan, the son of missionaries.

Wendy Staley Colbert's personal essays have been featured in Salon, *Whole Life Times*, Off Our Chests, and other publications. She is working on a memoir about her relationship with her brother who suffered from schizophrenia.

Jennifer Crowder left a Seattle corporation after seventeen years to write creative nonfiction. She holds an MA in English from the University of North Carolina. Her work appears in *We Came to Say* and *Hidden Lives: Coming Out on Mental Illness* (Brindle & Glass).

Robyne L. Curry began her career in newspapers, at a time when newspapers were still plentiful and powerful. She mourns their demise as a springboard for literary talents like Twain and Hemingway and Ephron. She hopes one day to add her name to the list.

Carmen D'Arcangelo began writing as a little girl growing up in Germany. In 2009 she graduated from the University of Washington's Memoir Certificate program. In 2011 "Grace" was published in *We Came to Say*. Recently she hosted an open mike Writers' Shabbat with her three children, who all write.

Elizabeth M. Economou, a freelance journalist, has had personal essays appear in *Newsweek*, *Newsday*, the *Seattle Times*, the *Seattle P-I*. and *Our Town*. In 2007, she returned to Seattle after a decade in New York City, where she worked as a staff business writer for CNBC. A former adjunct professor at Seattle University, she is a member of ASJA and working on a memoir about her time in NYC. *ElizabethmEconomou.com*.

Jean Engler is still a creative woman who enjoys working in many mediums, fabric, paper, photography, and writing. Single with no children of her own, she is a fantastic aunt to thirteen nephews and five nieces. Her writing goal is to create family stories to pass on for the next generation.

John Mace lives in Seattle with his two beagles. He has been writing since high school. John is a psychologist in private practice; gives lectures nationally and internationally on issues of psychology/physics/spirituality. He is currently writing two books: one about living with adults with autism and a personal memoir. *www.John-Mace.com.*

Dana Montanari began writing her memoir when she was fourteen years old on yellow legal pads. She holds a BS from Northeastern University and a memoir certificate from the University of Washington. She enjoys spending time with her husband of eighteen years and their two beautiful sons. TheImpatientQuilter.com.

Deli Moussavi-Bock was born in Iran and raised in California. Her long visit to Iran in 1978 launched an endless curiosity about cross-cultural family ties. She lives in the Northwest with her partner and two children. She has her hands full as a communication trainer, wannabe athlete, and often humbled new parent. Twitter Handle: DeliMBock.

Peggy A. Nagae is an author with degrees in Asian Studies, law, Spiritual Psychology and Illumination Sciences. She owns peggynagae consulting and coaches leaders to achieve strategic goals with greater grace and ease. Additionally, her expertise includes change, leadership, potentiating the human spirit at work, diversity, and inclusion. Contact her: peggy.nagae@gmail.com.

Theo Pauline Nestor teaches memoir writing for the University of Washington's Professional and Continuing Education's Certificate Program and coaches individual writers. She is the author of *How to Sleep Alone in a King-Size Bed* and has had personal essays published in the *New York Times*, The Huffington Post, *Brain, Child* magazine and numerous other publications. Her blog is *WritingIsMyDrink.com*.

Eleanor Owen, former reporter, costume designer, puppeteer and educator who taught Children's Drama at Lakeside and the University of Washington, is an advocate and co-founder of National Alliance on Mental Illness (NAMI). She is currently pitching her memoir, *Mama's Fireflies*, about growing up in an explosive Italian immigrant family during prohibition and the Great Depression

Julie Parks is a whimsical artist, photographer, and writer originally from New York City, Providence, and Boston. She lives on a quiet street in Seattle where she makes sharp observations with wit and humor often invisible to the naked eye.

Star Roberts is at work on *Hellsgate: Stories from A Northwest Childhood*. Her essay "Moving Away" is a PNWA Literary Contest Finalist for 2012. When not writing, she can be found reading, nesting, and mothering in the shadow of the Space Needle. She awaits good news at stargish@comcast.net.

Natalie Singer is a Seattle mother of two girls and a journalist who has written for newspapers, magazines, journals, blogs, and websites. In between school drop-offs and coffee binges she is the Web Editor at ParentMap.com. She is obsessed with cold sheets, scalding baths and self-referential nostalgia, whatever that is.

Joyce Tomlinson is currently a creative nonfiction student in the MFA program at Pacific University in Forest Grove, Oregon. A 2010 graduate of Antioch University Seattle, she completed the Certificate in Memoir Writing at the UW in 2011. Joyce lives in Snoqualmie.

Jeanne Verville has had careers in audiology, real estate, and law. She writes about the roles she's played during years of cultural change and essays on civility. Her essays have appeared in the 2010 and 2011 editions of *The Fallen Leal Anthology* and in *We Came to Say: A Collection of Memoir*. Jeanne's guiding principle is *carpe diem*. jeanneverville@comcast.net.

Kellini Walter lives in the Capitol Hill neighborhood of Seattle with her two daughters, two dogs, and three cats. For the past twenty years she has slowly come to understand that her career as a marketing professional is just a thinly veiled attempt to pursue her real love—writing. She has recently become an independent creative consultant.

Sue Wiedenfeld is a transplant from much sunnier California and has lived in Seattle since 1986. She began writing in 2008 after attending a life-coaching retreat to decide what to do next. She lives with her husband, seventeen-year-old son, and three-pound Chihuahua, Pepper. Much of her writing emerges from her longstanding interest in grief and loss.

Amber Wong is an environmental engineer and current MFA student in Creative Writing at Lesley University. Her essays, which explore generational perspectives on being Chinese American, have appeared in literary anthologies and online. Her recent essay "Swept Away" appeared in *The Fallen Leaf Anthology 2011*. She earned bachelor's and master's degrees from Stanford University.

Linda Zbigley was trained in writing through the UW's Memoir Certificate course 2009-2010 with Theo Pauline Nestor and the Genealogy and Family History course 2010-2011 with Sarah Thorson Little. Enlivened by dance movement therapy, she has been a science and ELL educator and organic farmer. Recently retired, she finds time to sing, write, and draw.